FOLK-DANCES

AND

SINGING GAMES

SWEDISH FOLK-DANCERS

FOLK-DANCES AND SINGING GAMES

TWENTY-SIX FOLK-DANCES

OF

The UNITED STATES, DENMARK, SWEDEN, RUSSIA, HUNGARY,
FINLAND, ITALY, CZECHO-SLOVAKIA,
ENGLAND, and SCOTLAND

WITH THE MUSIC, FULL DIRECTIONS FOR PERFORMANCE,
AND NUMEROUS ILLUSTRATIONS

DESCRIBED AND EDITED

BY

ELIZABETH BURCHENAL, B.A.

President American Folk-Dance Society; United States Member Inter-
national Commission on Folk-Arts; Executive Chairman National
Committee on Folk-Arts of the United States; Author: "American
Country Dances," "Dances of the People," "Folk-Dances from Old
Homelands," "Folk-Dances of Denmark," "Folk-Dances of Finland,"
"National Dances of Ireland," etc., etc.

REVISED EDITION

G. SCHIRMER, INC. , NEW YORK

Printed in the U. S. A.

PREFACE*

THE movement for folk-dancing in America is far more significant and complex than appears at first sight. There the love of beauty and rhythm, for which modern life seems to afford little opportunity, which expresses itself spontaneously in folk-dances containing the emotional experiences of the race. There is connected with the folk-dance a love of the open, of the vigor and joy of activity for its own sake, of coöperation with others in exercises of rhythmical beauty. There is the sense of balance and proportion that is related to all real art. More people can express themselves æsthetically through dancing than through any of the other arts. That is, a greater number of people can learn to dance than to sing, play, write poetry, paint pictures, or do anything else of an artistic character. So the folk-dancing movement is really a great æsthetic folk-movement.

But it has a meaning with reference to American life that is still deeper. We in America have recognized the value of the labor which the immigrants have brought to us, but we have not appreciated the wealth of tradition and experience which is embodied in the race-history of our immigrants; yet the great social composite that is developing in America not only is an embodiment of the physical abilities of the old countries, but also includes strands of their rich æsthetic life. To see a group of foreign-born people coöperating in bringing to us not only their labor, but their literature, their music, their folk-dancing, is to understand something of what is happening in connection with the folk-dance movement.

Miss Elizabeth Burchenal has an outstanding relation to this movement, not only through her personal enthusiasm, but through personal contact with people from various countries. She has learned the dances at first hand, from groups of people whom she discovered in this country and whose traditions she resurrected, as well as by visits abroad, where she has seen the dances performed in their original setting. Herself a skilled technical teacher, she has entered into the spirit of the dances—some of which are relatively unformed and even uncouth, others highly technical in form and meaning—and has selected those dances which were most obviously fitting to American conditions, and worked with distinguished success to introduce them under the difficult conditions of American life. Miss Burchenal has done a great service to the cause in acting as Chairman of the Committee on Folk-Dancing of the Playground Association of America. Her report to the Committee includes a list of selected dances suitable for grass playgrounds, for playgrounds with earth surfaces, for indoor playgrounds, for small children, for larger boys and girls, as well as for adults. It is one of the most important documents in connection with the practical conduct of the folk-dance movement in America.

Dancing is a language which may express that which is pure and true, or that which is debasing and degrading. Miss Burchenal's work is a definite, concrete force, making this language in America speak the word that is true and wholesome.

LUTHER H. GULICK.

June 10, 1909.

*PUBLISHERS' NOTE. The above Preface was written by Dr. Gulick for the original edition of **Folk-Dances and Singing Games,** published in 1909 when the folk-dance movement inaugurated by Miss Burchenal in the City of New York was four years old. Dr. Gulick was one of the founders of the American Folk-Dance Society in 1916, of which Miss Burchenal is president and director, under whose auspices a continuous program of educational promotion of the use of folk-dancing and appreciation of folk-arts in general has been carried on throughout the country. The Society was reorganized in 1929 to serve also as the United States Section of the International Commission on Folk-Arts.

GENERAL INDEX

CLASSIFIED INDEX

THE ILLUSTRATIONS

For the illustrations in this volume thanks are due to the following friends, of different nationalities, who posed for the photographs taken especially for it: Members of the Swedish Folk-Dance Society of New York; children of New York Club No. 1 and Brooklyn Club No. 2, of the Order of Vasa (American Swedish Organization); Mr. William Cameron; Mr. and Mrs. Carl Hansen; and members of the Finnish Folk-Dance Society of Brooklyn.

FOLK-DANCES

AND

SINGING GAMES

JOHN BROWN

(United States)

1. O Susanna

2. Two Buffalo Girls

JOHN BROWN*
(United States)

This is one of the numerous American country dances which has no specified melody associated with it, the fiddler playing any of the usual country dance tunes that may suit his fancy—usually a combination of several such tunes. Two good typical pieces are given here with a simple arrangement for piano—"O Susanna" and "Buffalo Girls."

Any number of couples form a circle all facing the center, with each girl on the right of her partner. In the center stands an extra man who is "John Brown"; or (according to the size of the circle and the number of dancers) there may be several John Browns. [Diag. 1.] A leader calls the changes of the dance which are indicated below in quotation-marks.

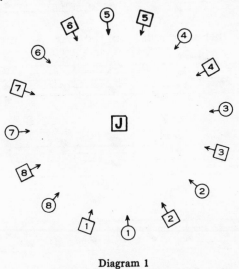

Diagram 1

"Ladies Forward and Salute John Brown"

(**Meas. 1-2.**) While the men stand still, the girls advance four steps toward John Brown making a slight courtesy to him on the fourth count, then (**Meas. 3-4**) retire four steps to their places.

"Now the Gents"

(**Meas. 5-6.**) While the girls stand still, the men advance four steps and "salute" John Brown—usually by slapping him on the back or rumpling his hair—then (**Meas. 7-8**) retire four steps to their places.

"Grand Right and Left"

(**Meas. 1-8.**) All dance the "Grand Right and Left." As soon as this begins, John Brown joins in with the others. There is no set number of measures for this and it is continued until the leader sees fit to call the next change.

The "Grand Right and Left" is danced as follows: Partners face each other, taking right hands; then moving forward past each other, they release right hands and each gives left hand to the next dancer, passes that one and gives right hand to the next, and so on until the call for the next change.

"Promenade All"

(**Meas. 9-16.**) At this call, each man secures the girl nearest him as a partner, if he can. With each girl on the right of her new partner and arm in arm with him, couples march around the circle in the direction opposite to the hands of the clock. The man (or men) who failed to secure a partner now becomes John Brown and takes his place in the center of the circle. The "Promenade" continues until the call "Ladies Forward" when the dance begins again. It is repeated in this manner as often as desired, or until the music stops. The leader sometimes brings it to a finish by calling "Swing your partner and promenade to seats" at which partners join both hands and swing in place.

---

*Another version of this American country dance, as found in Connecticut, is given in American Country Dances, Vol. I, by Burchenal, published by G. Schirmer (Inc.).

CAPTAIN JINKS

(United States)

Cap - tain Jinks came home last night, The gen-tle-man pass - es to the right,

Swing your part - ner so po - lite, For that's the style in the Ar - my!

Fine

All join hands and cir - cle left, Cir - cle left, cir - cle left,

All join hands and cir - cle left, For that's the style in the ar - my.

CAPTAIN JINKS

(United States)

This is one of the United States folk-games, or song-dances known as "Play Party Games." True to folk-form, it has numerous variants found in different localities. The tune is the familiar one of "Captain Jinks of the Horse Marines" and the words are a jingle descriptive of the action. A piano arrangement of the melody is given here for convenience though in its original form there is no instrumental accompaniment to the game, the players providing the music by singing the song.

A.

Captain Jinks came home last night,
Gentleman passes to the right,
Swing your partner so polite,
For that's the style in the army!

B.

All join hands and circle left,
Circle left, circle left,
All join hands and circle left,
For that's the style in the army!

Any number of couples join hands in a ring with each girl on the right of her partner and all facing the center. [Diag. 1.] The step used throughout the game is the usual country dance step, an easy springy, walking step, two to each measure of the music.

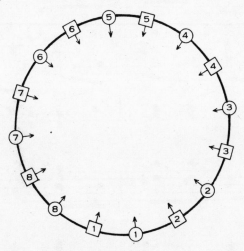

Diagram 1

A.

(**Meas. 1-2.**) While singing "Captain Jinks came home last night," all balance, that is, take two steps forward toward the center of the circle, then two steps backward.

(**Meas. 3-4.**) While singing "Gentleman passes to the right," partners face each other joining right hands and go forward past each other releasing hands as they pass. [Diag. 2.] Each boy now finds himself face to face with a new partner.

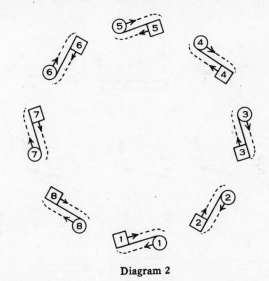

Diagram 2

(**Meas. 5-8.**) While singing "Swing your partner so polite, For that's the style in the army!", each boy joins both hands with his new partner, swings her around in place, turning in the direction of the hands of the clock, with eight steps, and finishes by placing her on his right side.

B.

(**Meas. 9-16.**) While singing "All join hands and circle left," etc., all join hands in a ring again and circle to the left with sixteen steps.

Repeat the whole game from the beginning (**A**) and continue in this manner as long as desired, with each boy progressing to and swinging a new partner at each repetition of the game.

FOLK-DANCES AND SINGING GAMES

SHOEMAKERS' DANCE

(Danish)

SHOEMAKERS' DANCE

(Danish)

The music consists of two parts of eight measures each.

In fitting the steps to the music, each measure should be counted thus: "**One, and, two, and.**"

The dancers form a double circle, partners standing side by side facing in the same direction.

A.

Partners face each other, Number One facing the centre of the circle, Number Two facing outward.

(**Meas. 1.**) With fists tightly clenched in front of the chest, revolve them around each other as quickly as possible, moving them inward, upward,

Figure 1

and outward. [Fig. 1.] (This represents the winding of the thread.)

(**Meas. 2.**) Without pausing, reverse, winding as quickly as possible in the opposite direction.

(**Meas. 3.**) Jerk the elbows back quickly and vigorously twice (**one, and**) (**two, and**). (This represents pulling the thread.)

(**Meas. 4.**) With fists tightly clenched strike the left one smartly with the right one three times (**one,**

and, two), pause (**and**). (This represents driving the pegs.)

(**Meas. 5-8.**) Repeat the steps of Meas. 1-4.

Figure 2

B.

Partners face in the same direction, with left side toward the centre of the circle, and with inside hands joined and outside hands on hips, all polka around the circle. The polka is executed as follows:

(**Meas. 1.**) Both step forward with outside foot, at the same time turning slightly toward partner and swinging the inside joined hands backward (**one**).

Close the inside foot to the outside foot (**and**).

Step forward with the outside foot (**two**).

Hop on the outside foot (**and**).

(**Meas. 2.**) Repeat, beginning with the inside foot, at the same time turning slightly away from partner and swinging joined hands forward.

(**Meas. 3-8.**) Continue the same (or partners take the ordinary position for round dancing, and polka around the room during **B**).

The Polka should be danced lightly on the toes with much spring and life.

FOLK-DANCES AND SINGING GAMES

MOUNTAIN MARCH

(Danish)

MOUNTAIN MARCH

(Danish)

The music consists of two parts of sixteen measures each. In fitting the steps to the music, each measure should be counted thus: "**One, two, three.**"

The dance is performed in groups of three, all moving forward and around the room from right to left.

In each group of three, Number One stands in front with a handkerchief or scarf in either hand; Number Two and Number Three stand side by side directly behind him, Number Two on the left, Number Three on the right, with inside hands joined and outside hand of each grasping the end of the nearest handkerchief, thus forming a triangle.

The Step

The step used throughout the dance is as follows:

First measure: Step forward on the right foot (**one**); swing the left foot forward (**two**); hop on the right foot (**three**).

Second measure: Step forward on the left foot (**one**); swing the right foot forward (**two**); hop on the left foot (**three**); and so on.

A.

(**Meas. 1-16.**) Beginning with the right foot, all dance forward around the room [Diag. 1], accenting slightly the first count of each measure.

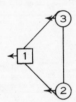

Diagram 1

B.

(**Meas. 1-2.**) Number One, bending forward, dances backward, stamping on the first step, and [Diag. 2] passes under the joined hands of Numbers Two and Three.

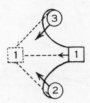

Diagram 2

(During Measures 1 and 2, Numbers Two and Three dance in place.)

(**Meas. 3-4.**) Number Two dances across in front of Number One, and turns inward once around in place under Number One's right arm.

(**Meas. 5-6.**) Number Three turns inward once around in place under Number One's right arm.

(**Meas. 7-8.**) Number One turns once around to the right under his own right arm.

This should bring the three back to their original position. In executing this figure, each should continue dancing in place while the others execute their part.

(**Meas. 9-16.** Repeat the same, Number One omitting the stamp on first count.

This dance is said to represent two mountain-climbers with their guide. Number One, being the guide, should keep well in advance of Numbers Two and Three in **A**, and should appear to be drawing them after him, glancing back occasionally first over one shoulder and then over the other as if to see how they are getting on.

DANCE OF GREETING*

(Danish)

* By permission of Miss MARI HOFER.

DANCE OF GREETING

(Danish)

The music consists of two parts, each of which contains eight measures.

In fitting the steps to the music, each measure should be counted thus:—"**One, and, two, and.**"

The dancers form a single circle with hands joined, partners standing side by side, and all facing toward the centre of the circle.

A.

(**Meas. 1.**) All clap own hands together (**one**), clap again (**and**). With both hands lowered diagonally forward and outward lift the skirts lightly and, with the foot farthest from the partner, step to the side, at the same time pointing the foot nearest the partner and making a deep courtesy to partner (**two, and**).

(**Meas. 2.**) Sway the weight on to the foot nearest partner, at the same time clapping the hands twice as before (**one, and**). With the weight on the foot nearest partner, turn away from partner, pointing the foot farthest from the partner and making a deep courtesy to the dancer on the other side (**two, and**).

(**Meas. 3.**) With the hands still lifting the skirts, all face toward the centre of the circle and stamp with the foot farthest away from partner (**one, and**); then stamp the other foot (**two, and**).

(**Meas. 4.**) With three light running-steps, turn away from partner, once around in place (**one, and, two**), pause (**and**).

(**Meas. 5-8.**) Repeat all.

B.

(**Meas. 1-4.**) All join hands, closing the circle, face toward the left, and, starting with the left foot, dance lightly around the circle, making four running-steps to each measure.

(**Meas. 5-8.**) Without pausing, all face the other way and dance around the circle to the right.

It should be remembered that the movements in **A** represent a happy greeting to all the dancers, and the courtesies should be made to express that meaning.

B represents the pleasure of all being together, and should be rollicking and full of fun.

FOLK-DANCES AND SINGING GAMES

THE ACE OF DIAMONDS

(Danish)

THE ACE OF DIAMONDS

(Danish)

The music of this dance consists of three strains of eight measures each.

In fitting the steps to the music, each measure should be counted thus: "**One, and, two, and.**"

The dancers form a double circle.

A.

Partners face each other, Number One of each couple facing the centre of the circle, Number Two facing outward.

(**Meas. 1-4.**) All clap their own hands together once smartly (**one**).

Immediately hook right elbows and, starting with the left foot, swing partner around, making *two* slow running-steps to each measure. [Fig. 1.]

(**Meas. 5-8.**) Without pausing, clap hands again (**one**), hook left elbows and swing partner around the other way.

Finish in original position, facing each other with arms folded (or hands on hips).

B.

(**Meas. 1.**) Number One steps forward on the right foot (**one, and**).

Hop on the right foot (**two, and**).

(**Meas. 2.**) Number One steps forward on left foot (**one, and**).

Hop on left foot (**two, and**).

(**Meas. 3-4.**) Number One continues the same step, moving forward toward the centre of the circle.

Number Two at the same time executes the same step, but moving backward toward centre of circle, keeping close to and face to face with Number One.

(**Meas. 5-8.**) Repeat the same steps, but Number One going backward and Number Two going forward, both moving out from the centre of the circle. (Instead of the "step hop" described, **B** may be danced with a waltz balance step.)

(**Meas. 1-8.**) Partners turn so as to stand side by side, both facing in the same direction, with inside hands joined and outside hands on hips, and polka around the circle as described in **B** of the Shoemakers' Dance (or partners may take the ordinary position for round dancing and polka around the room).

Figure 1

WASHING CLOTHES

(Swedish Singing Game)

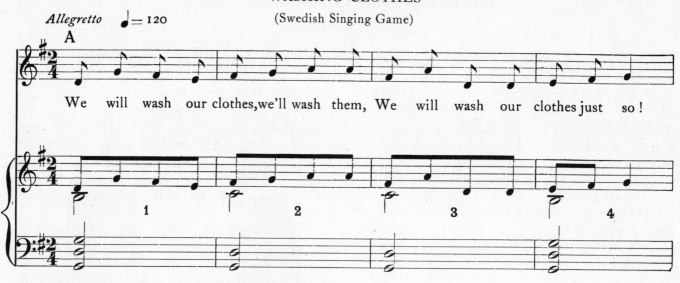

We will wash our clothes, we'll wash them, We will wash our clothes just so!

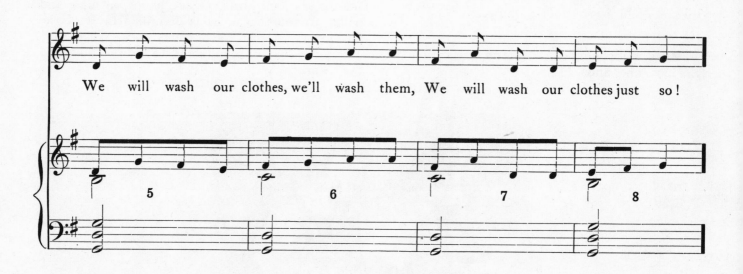

We will wash our clothes, we'll wash them, We will wash our clothes just so!

Tra, la, la la la, Tra, la, la la la, Tra, la, la la la, Tra, la, la!

WASHING CLOTHES

(Swedish Singing Game)

The music consists of two parts of eight measures each.

In fitting the movements to the music, each measure should be counted thus: **"One, two."**

The dancers stand in two parallel lines facing each other, Number Ones in the left line, Number Twos in the right line.

1. WASHING THE CLOTHES
A.

(**Meas. 1-8.**) The dancers all bend forward and rub the fist of one hand on the palm of the other, as if washing clothes. [Fig. 1.]

Figure 1

B.

(**Meas. 1.**) With hands on the hips, touch the left foot across in front of the right foot (**one**). [Fig. 2.]

Replace the left foot so that the heels are together (**two**).

(**Meas. 2.**) Touch the right foot across in front of the left foot (**one**).

Heels together (**two**).

(**Meas. 3-6.**) Continue the same.

(**Meas. 7-8.**) With three stamps (**right, left, right**) turn once around to the right in place, and at the same time clap the hands together three times (**one, two—Meas. 7**), (**one—Meas. 8**) and pause in original position (**two—Meas. 8**).

In every figure of the dance the steps done to **B** are the same.

Figure 2

2. CLAPPING THE CLOTHES
A.

(**Meas. 1.**) Number Two of each couple extends hands forward toward partner with palms turned up. [Fig. 3.] Number One at the same time, with palms down, claps Number Two's hands (**one**); all clap own hands together (**two**).

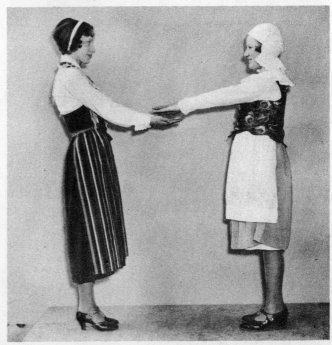

Figure 3

(**Meas. 2.**) Number One extends hands forward with palms up, and Number Two with palms down claps Number One's hands (**one**); all clap own hands together (**two**).

(**Meas. 3-8.**) Continue the same.

B.

(**Meas. 1-8.**)⸱ Execute the second part as described in B of the first figure.

3. RINSING THE CLOTHES

A.

(**Meas. 1.**) With both hands joined [Fig. 4], partners swing both arms to the side farthest from the front of the line (**one**), then swing arms down to the starting position (**two**).

Figure 4

(**Meas. 2.**) Swing the arms to the other side, toward the front end of the line (**one**), then bring them back to the starting position (**two**).

(**Meas. 3-8.**) Continue the same.

B.

(**Meas. 1-8.**) As described in B of the first figure.

4. WRINGING THE CLOTHES

A.

(**Meas. 1.**) Partners join both hands and swing the arms farthest from the front of the line-up over their heads [Fig. 5], and at the same time both twist the body to the side away from the front of the line (**one**), and bring hands back to starting position (**two**).

(**Meas. 2.**) Repeat same, swinging other arms overhead and twisting toward the front of the line (**one**), and return to starting position (**two**).

(**Meas. 3-8.**) Continue the same.

Figure 5

B.

(**Meas. 1-8.**) As described in B of the first figure.

5. HANGING THE CLOTHES

A.

(**Meas. 1.**) All reach upward as if hanging up clothes on the line (**one, two**).

(**Meas. 2.**) Bring the arms sideward and down (**one, two**).

(**Meas. 3-8.**) Continue the same.

B.

(**Meas. 1-8.**) As described in B of the first figure.

6. STRETCHING THE CLOTHES

A.

(**Meas. 1.**) Partners join both hands, and in the first couple Number One runs three steps backward [Fig. 6], pulling with him Number Two, who at the same time runs three steps forward (**one, and, two**), then stands still (**and**).

(**Meas. 2.**) Repeat the same, but with Number Two running three steps backward to place, pulling Number One.

(**Meas. 3-8.**) Continue the same.

The second couple execute the same step, but move in the opposite direction, Number Two pulling backward in the first measure. The odd-numbered couples all execute step as described for the first couple; the even-numbered execute the step as described for the second couple.

B.

(**Meas. 1-8.**) As described in B of the first figure.

7. MANGLING THE CLOTHES

A.

(**Meas. 1.**) Partners join both hands; Number

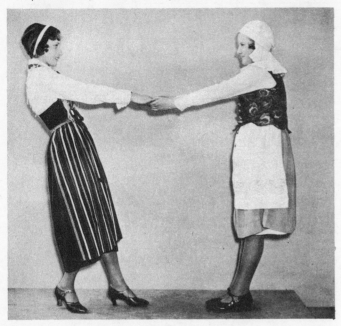

Figure 6

One bows forward, keeping the knees straight, and remains in that position. At the same time Number Two, with head erect, bends the knees and holds that position (**one, two**).

(**Meas. 2.**) Number One, with head erect, bends the knees and remains in that position. At the same time Number Two, with straightened knees, bows forward and remains in that position (**one, two**).

(**Meas. 3-8.**) Continue the same.

B.

(**Meas. 1-8.**) As described in B, first figure.

8. CONCLUSION

A.

(**Meas. 1-8.**) All the dancers join hands, forming a single circle, and with running steps dance around circle to left, two steps to each measure.

B.

(**Meas. 1-8.**) Repeat in the opposite direction, and finish with three stamps.

This series represents the process of washing and drying the clothes, with a dance at the end to express pleasure at the completion of the work. During each figure the movements are made vigorously to the accompaniment of the appropriate verse, the word fitting the action.

1 (A).

We will wash our clothes, we'll wash them,
We will wash our clothes just so! (*Repeat.*)

1 (B).

Tra, la, la la la,
Tra, la, la la la,
Tra, la, la la la,
Tra, la, la!

2 (A).

We will clap our clothes, we'll clap them,
We will clap our clothes just so! *etc.*

2 (B).

Tra, la, la la la, *etc.*

3. We will rinse our clothes, we'll rinse them.
4. We will wring our clothes, we'll wring them.
5. We will hang our clothes, we'll hang them.
6. We will stretch our clothes, we'll stretch them.
7. We will mangle our clothes, we'll mangle them.

TAILORS' DANCE

(Swedish Singing Game)

A heart of hap - pi - ness is mine, To make a man, takes

tai - lors nine, A heart of hap - pi - ness is mine, To make a man, takes

tai - lors nine, With thim - ble, scis - sors, nee - dle, too, And thread run

through, With thim - ble, scis - sors, nee - dle, too, And thread run through.

TAILORS' DANCE

(Swedish Singing Game)

The music consists of two parts of eight measures each.

In fitting the steps to the music, each measure should be counted thus: **"One, and, two, and."**

The dancers stand in couples, but in a single circle with all hands joined.

A.

(**Meas. 1-8.**) Beginning with the left foot, all polka forward around the circle from right to left, making one polka step (see p. 18) to each measure. [Fig. 1.]

Figure 1

B.

(**Meas. 1.**) Partners face each other. With left hand on hip, the right arm raised to the side with elbow shoulder-high and forearm bent at right angles so that the hand is pointing upward with all fingers closed except the index and middle fingers, each dancer touches the left heel to the side with the toes raised from the ground (**one, and**), then replaces left foot so that the heels are together (**two, and**). At the same time, separate and bring together the two extended fingers of the raised hand as if they were a pair of scissors. Do this twice (**one, and, two, and**).

(**Meas. 2.**) Repeat.

(**Meas. 3-4.**) Partners join both hands, and extend them sideways horizontally, and with four walking steps turn partner in place.

(**Meas. 5-6.**) Same as in measures 1 and 2, except that all touch the **right** heel sideways and make the scissors movements with two fingers of the **left** hand.

(**Meas. 7-8.**) Turn partner as in **Meas. 3-4.**

At the end of the eighth measure all immediately join hands again in a single circle, and repeat the dance, this time moving around the circle from left to right during **A.**

As they dance, the children sing the words of the game.

A.

A heart of happiness is mine,
  To make a man, takes tailors nine,
A heart of happiness is mine,
  To make a man, takes tailors nine.

B.

With thimble, scissors, needle too,
  And thread run through,
With thimble, scissors, needle too,
  And thread run through.

I SEE YOU

(Swedish Singing Game)

I see you, I see you, Tra la la la la la la la, I see you, I see you, Tra la la la la la! You see me and I see you, Then you take me and I'll take you; You see me and I see you, Then you take me and I'll take you.

I SEE YOU

(Swedish Singing Game)

The music consists of two parts of eight measures each.

In fitting the movements to the music of **A,** each measure should be counted thus: **"One, two."**

In fitting the steps to the music of **B,** each measure should be counted thus: **"One, and, two, and."**

The dancers form in two double lines, which face toward each other and are about six feet apart.

In each of these double lines, Number One stands with hands on hips; Number Two stands behind Number One with hands on Number One's shoulders.

A.

(Meas. 1.) Number Two leans head to the left, and looks over partner's shoulder across at Number Two of the opposite couple (**one**), pause in this position (**two**).

(**Meas. 2.**) With a quick movement lean head to right and look across at Number Two of opposite couple (**one**), pause in this position (**two**). [**Fig. 1.**]

tion, but with positions changed so that Number One is standing behind Number Two.

The whole dance is then repeated with Number

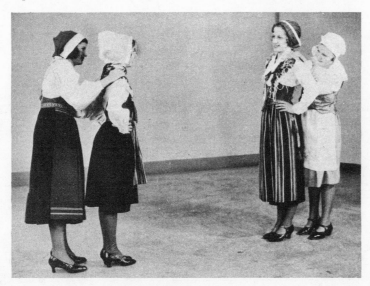

Figure 1

(**Meas. 3.**) With quick staccato movements look to the left (**one**), to the right (**two**).

(**Meas. 4.**) To the left (**one**), pause in this position (**two**).

(**Meas. 5-8.**) Repeat movement of **Meas. 1-4**, leaning head first to right.

B.

(**Meas. 1-4.**) On the first note of the first measure, all clap own hands together sharply and, at the same time, Number Two springs forward to the left of partner and grasps the hands of Number Two from the opposite side, swinging vigorously around to the left with a sliding step, making two slides with the left foot to each measure.

Ones looking across at each other.

These are the words which accompany the dance:

A.

I see you, I see you,
Tra la la la la la la la,
I see you, I see you,
Tra la la la la la!

B.

You see me and I see you,
Then you take me and I'll take you;
You see me and I see you,
Then you take me and I'll take you.

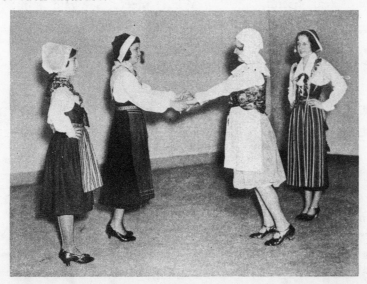

Figure 2

(**Meas. 5-8.**) On the first note of the fifth measure, all clap hands together again sharply, immediately grasp the hands of own partners, and swing around to the left as before.

At the end of **B**, all resume the original forma-

In the first part of the dance, the movement of the head should be quick and bird-like.

In the second part the dancers should grasp hands firmly and lean away from each other, making the swing very vigorous.

THE FIRST OF MAY

(Swedish Singing Game)

To - day's the first of May,   To - day's the first of May, May, May, To -

day's the first of May,   To - day's the first of May.   Good -

bye, good - bye, dear friend,   We'll meet a - gain some day, some day, We'll

meet a - gain some day,   Be - fore the first of May.

THE FIRST OF MAY

(Swedish Singing Game)

The music consists of eight measures, which are played twice; the first time for **A**, the second time for **B**.

The dancers form a double circle, partners standing side by side with inside hands joined, outside hands on hips, all facing ready to move around the circle, Number One outside on the left, Number Two inside on the right.

In fitting the steps to the music, each measure should be counted thus: **"One, and, two, and."**

A.

(**Meas. 1-8.**) Beginning with the inside foot and swinging the arms forward, all polka forward around the circle as described in the "Ace of Diamonds," and the "Shoemakers' Dance."

B.

(**Meas. 1-2.**) Partners, facing each other, shake each other's right hand three times (first measure: **one, and, two, and**) (second measure: **one, and**), pause (**two, and**).

(**Meas. 3-8.**) Numbers One and Two both make a quarter-turn to their own right and march or skip around the circle, with a clap of the hands and a stamp on the first note of the third measure, the outside circle moving in the same direction as during

A, the inside circle moving in the opposite direction, until Number One passes his partner and meets the dancer who is next behind her.

At the end of **B**, all face in same direction as at beginning of dance, and join inside hands with new partners.

The dance is repeated any number of times desired, each time with a new partner.

To-day's the first of May,
To-day's the first of May, May, May,
To-day's the first of May,
To-day's the first of May!

Good-bye, good-bye, dear friend,
We'll meet again some day, some day,
We'll meet again some day,
Before the first of May.

During the first part of the dance, the polka is taken very lightly and joyously, with the arms swinging back and forth.

During the second part, the three hand-shakings are made on the words "Good-**bye**, good-**bye**, dear **friend**," and the stamp is made on the first **"meet."**

This dance may be used for a great variety of special occasions, the names of which may be substituted for "The First of May."

CAROUSEL (MERRY-GO-ROUND)
(Swedish Singing Game)

A *Moderato con moto* ♩=84

Pret-ty maid-en, sweet and gay, Car-ou-sel is run - ning,

It will run till eve - ning: Lit-tle ones a nick-el, Big ones a dime. Hur-ry

B *Faster.* ♩=108

up! Get a *mate!* Or you'll *sure*-ly be too *late!* Ha ha ha!

Hap-py are we, An-der-son, and Pe-ter-son, and Lünd - strom, and me!

CAROUSEL

(Swedish Singing Game)

This dance represents the "Merry-go-round," or "Flying Horses." The dancers form a double circle, standing in couples, both facing toward centre of circle. The front ones of all couples join hands in a circle; the back ones place their hands on their partners' shoulders.

The music consists of two parts. The first part contains seven measures; the second part, eight.

In fitting the steps to the music, each measure should be counted thus: **"One, two, three, four."**

A.

During **A** dancers move toward the left with a slow sliding step, as follows:

(**Meas. 1.**) Make a long slide to the left with the left foot (**one**), close the right foot to the left (**two**). Repeat (**three, four**).

Figure 1

(**Meas. 2-7.**) Continue through the seven measures of **A**, but, during the sixth and seventh measures, make stamps instead of slides.

During the sixth and seventh measures, the time is accelerated slightly.

B.

(**Meas. 1-4.**) Still moving to the left, with the time slightly accelerated, as in the two preceding measures, execute the same step as described in the first measure of **A**, but in **double time**, that is, making four slides to each measure instead of two. [Fig. 1.]

(**Meas. 5-8.**) Repeat, sliding to the right.

At the end of **B**, partners immediately change places, those who were behind now standing in front with hands joined, the others behind with hands on partners' shoulders.

The whole dance is then repeated.

The words are sung by the dancers as they dance. The four stamps in the sixth and seventh measures of **A** are made on the words, **"up, mate, surely, late."**

In the chorus, "Ha ha ha!" should be shouted heartily with heads thrown back.

A.

Pretty maiden, sweet and gay,
    Carousel is running,
    It will run till evening:
Little ones a nickel, big ones a dime.
    Hurry **up**! get a **mate**!
    Or you'll **sure**ly be too **late**!

B.

Ha ha ha! Happy are we,
Anderson, and Peterson, and Lündstrom, and me!
Ha ha ha! Happy are we,
Anderson, and Peterson, and Lündstrom, and me!

During the first part of "Carousel" the merry-go-round is supposed to be just starting, and moves slowly; in the second part it is in full swing, and the fun is at its height.

MA'S LITTLE PIGS

(Swedish Singing Game)

Ma's lit - tle pigs we're all of us, . . . All of us, . . .

all of us, . . . Ma's lit - tle pigs we're all of us, . . .

All of us, . . . and me, too, Me, too, and you, too!

MA'S LITTLE PIGS

(Swedish Singing Game)

The music consists of one strain of ten measures. The dancers form a single circle with hands joined, partners standing side by side, Number One on the left, Number Two on the right, and all facing inward toward the leader, who stands in centre of circle and starts the singing. The dancers are also counted off in fours around the circle, from left to right.

In fitting the movements to the music, each measure should be counted thus: **One, two, three.**

I.

(**Meas. 1-7.**) Beginning with the left foot, all run around the circle to the left, making three steps to each measure and stamping on the first count of each measure.

(**Meas. 8.**) Number One places hands on hips and faces partner, and Number Two, with feet together and knees straight, bows with left hand on hip and right hand on chest. This is done as they sing "Me, too."

(**Meas. 9.**) Number Two places hands on hips, and Number One bows to partner, with left hand on hip and right hand on chest; this is done as they sing "Me, too."

(**Meas. 10.**) All quickly face the leader in the centre, with hands joined in a single circle, and all bow to the leader. This is done as they sing "You, too."

2.

(**Meas. 1-10.**) Repeat 1; except that during the first to seventh measures all run around the circle to the right instead of to the left.

3.

(**Meas. 1-7.**) Dividing into groups of four all the groups, with the exception of the first four, join hands, each group forming a small circle. The dancers in these small circles run around to the left, and at the same time the first four, with hands joined in a string, run to the left all the way around the large circle, winding in and out among the small circles. The first eight measures of the music are repeated without bowing until the first four dancers are back in place.

(**Meas. 8-10.**) Then all quickly form a single circle again, and bow to each other and to the leader, as before. Repeat until each group of four in turn has wound in and out around the circle in the same way.

4.

(**Meas. 1-7.**) Partners face each other with both hands joined and, with running steps, swing each other around in place.

(**Meas. 8-9.**) Form a single circle, and bow to each other as before.

(**Meas. 10.**) Bow to the leader, as before.

The words are sung at the same time.

Ma's little pigs we're all of us,
All of us, all of us,
Ma's little pigs we're all of us,
All of us, and me, too,
Me, too, and you, too!

GRANDMA'S OLD SPARROW

(Swedish Singing Game)

1. Grand - ma drove her spar - row hitch'd up to the cart, And how to drive she could not tell, O! Grand - ma drove her spar - row hitch'd up to the cart, And how to drive she could not tell, O!

2. Then the par - son start - ed out to drive the spar - row, How to drive he could not tell, O! Then the par - son start - ed out to drive the spar - row, How to drive he could not tell, O!

This way they stumbled, that way they stumbled, Down in the ditch they fell, O!

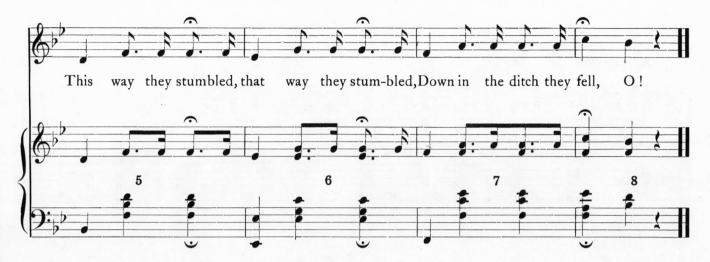

This way they stumbled, that way they stum-bled, Down in the ditch they fell, O!

GRANDMA'S OLD SPARROW

(Swedish Singing Game)

The music consists of two parts of eight measures each. In fitting the movements, each measure should be counted thus: "One, two, three."

The dancers all form in a single circle, with hands joined.

A.

(Meas. 1-7.) All run around the circle to the left, beginning with the left foot, making three steps to each measure and stamping on the first count of each measure.

(Meas. 8.) All stamp with the right foot, and at the same time face toward centre of circle (one), stamp with left foot (two), pause (three).

B.

(Meas. 1.) With hands still joined, and facing the centre of the circle, all make a vigorous lunge diagonally forward to the left, with the left foot, and let the head and shoulders drop forward (one, two). Replace the left foot so that the heels are together, and return to erect position (three).

(Meas. 2.) All lunge to the right in the same manner.

(Meas. 3.) Bend the knees (one, two), jump straight up as high as possible from the ground (three).

(Meas. 4.) Land with feet together, head erect, knees bent, and sitting on heels (one, two), straighten the knees and return to standing position (three).

(Meas. 5-8.) Repeat the same.

Repeat the whole dance, running around the circle to the **right** during **A**.

The words of the dance are as follows:

A.

Grandma drove her sparrow hitched up to the cart,
 And how to drive she could not tell, O!
Grandma drove her sparrow hitched up to the cart,
 And how to drive she could not tell, O!

B.

This way they stumbled, that way they stumbled,
 Down in the ditch they fell, O!
This way they stumbled, that way they stumbled,
 Down in the ditch they fell, O!

A.

Then the parson started out to drive the sparrow,
 How to drive he could not tell, O!
Then the parson started out to drive the sparrow,
 How to drive he could not tell, O!

B.

This way they stumbled, that way they stumbled,
 Down in the ditch they fell, O!
This way they stumbled, that way they stumbled,
 Down in the ditch they fell, O!

OXDANSEN

(Swedish)

OXDANSEN

(Swedish)

This is danced in Sweden by men only, and represents a mock fight. All the movements should be made with this meaning.

There is a salutation before the fight, then treading on toes, jostling elbows, wrestling, and boxing. The vigorous side-step at the end of each figure should be done with bravado.

The music consists of three strains of eight measures each.

In fitting the steps to the music, each measure should be counted "One, two, three, four."

It should be remembered that in each step, slow movements are made during the first strain; during the second strain these same movements are repeated quickly; and the side-step done to the third strain is the same in each figure throughout the dance.

The dancers stand in two lines facing each other, about three feet apart, with their hands on their hips. All those in the left-hand line are numbered **One,** and their partners are numbered **Two.**

I. A.

(**Meas. 1.**) Dancers stand still.

(**Meas. 2.**) On the first count of the second measure Number One, with knees straight, makes a deep bow to Number Two and returns to standing position. At the same time, Number Two, with body erect, bends both knees and immediately returns to standing position. [Fig. 1.]

(**Meas. 3.**) Dancers stand still.

(**Meas. 4.**) On the first count of the fourth measure Number Two makes the bow and Number One bends the knees.

(**Meas. 5-8.**) Repeat the same.

B.

On the first count of the first measure, Number One makes a quick bow, Number Two makes a quick bend of the knees. On the third count of the same measure, Number One makes a quick bend of the knees, Number Two makes a quick bow.

(**Meas. 2-8.**) Continue the same.

Figure 1

Figure 4

C.

(**Meas. 1.**)   Number One clenches fists close in front of chest [Fig. 2], with elbows raised shoulder-high, and on the first count turns the head to the right, throws the arms vigorously sideways [Fig. 3] and with the right leg extended and raised to the side leaps to the right (**one, two**), then steps to the side with right foot (**three**), and closes left foot to right (**four**).

(**Meas. 2.**)   Step again to the right with the right foot (**one, two**), stamp the left foot to the right and at the same time bring the hands back to the chest with a quick jerk and turn the face toward partner (**three, four**).

(**Meas. 3-4.**)   Repeat the same step with the other foot, and moving to the left.

(**Meas. 5-6.**)   Repeat to the right.

(**Meas. 7-8.**)   Repeat to the left.

(Number Two at the same time executes the same steps, but starting with the left foot, so that the dancers move in the same direction, keeping face to face.)

2. A.

(**Meas. 1.**)   With hands on hips, dancers stand still.

(**Meas. 2.**)   Both spring and place the right foot forward [Fig. 4] (**one**), hold this position (**two, three, four**).

(**Meas. 3.**)   Dancers stand still in this position.

(**Meas. 4.**)   Both spring and place the left foot forward (**one**), hold this position (**two, three, four**).

(**Meas. 5-8.**)   Repeat the same.

B.

(**Meas. 1-8.**)   Execute the same movements, making two movements to a measure, instead of one.

C.

Same as C of first figure.

3. A.

(**Meas. 1.**)   With hands on hips, dancers stand still.

(**Meas. 2.**)   Each dancer turns a quarter-turn to the left, so that the right elbows touch, and each looks directly at the other (**one**); hold this position (**two, three, four**).

(**Meas. 3.**)   Hold this position.

(**Meas. 4.**)   Both make a half-turn to the right, so that the left elbows touch (**one**); hold this position (**two, three, four**).   [Fig. 5.]

(**Meas. 5-8.**)   Repeat the same.

Figure 2   Figure 3

B.

(**Meas. 1-8.**)   Execute the same movements, making two movements to a measure, instead of one.

C.

Same as C of first figure.

4. A.

(**Meas. 1.**)   With hands on hips and right foot advanced, partners stand still.

(**Meas. 2.**)   Number One makes a vigorous movement with the right arm as if boxing Number Two's left ear [Fig. 6], and immediately replaces right hand on hip; at the same time Number Two claps own palms together down in front, making a sharp noise (**one**), immediately replacing hands on hips (**two, three, four**).

(**Meas. 3.**)   Both stand still.

(**Meas. 4.**)   Same as Meas. 2, but Number Two strikes and Number One claps hands (**one**); and replace hands on hips as in first measure (**two, three, four**).

(**Meas. 5-8.**)   Repeat the same.

C.

Same as C of first figure.

5. A.

(**Meas. 1.**)   Dancers stand still, with right foot advanced, each placing his right hand upon the other's head, both heads erect.

(**Meas. 2.**)   Number One pulls Number Two's head forward (**one**); holds this position (**two, three, four**).

(**Meas 3.**)   The dancers hold same position.

(**Meas. 4.**)   Number Two pulls Number One's head forward, at the same time making own erect [Fig. 7] (**one**); hold this position (**two, three, four**).

(**Meas. 5-8.**)   Repeat the same.

B.

Execute the same movements, making two movements to a measure.

C.

Same as C of first figure.

Figure 7   Figure 6

B.

(**Meas. 1-8.**)   Execute the same movements, making two movements ·to a measure, and not re-placing the hands on hips between movements.

6. A.

(**Meas. 1.**)   With right foot advanced, hands on hips, dancers stand still.

(**Meas. 2.**)   Both strike diagonally forward with

the right fist clenched, thrusting under partner's right arm (**one**); hold this position (**two, three, four**). [Fig. 8.]

(**Meas. 3.**)   Hold same position.

(**Meas. 4.**)   Replace the right hand on hip and at the same time thrust with the left fist (**one**); hold this position (**two, three, four**).

(**Meas. 5-8.**)   Repeat the same.

B.

(**Meas. 1-8.**)   Execute the same movements in quick time, without replacing hands on hips, and making two thrusts to a measure.

C.

Same as C of first figure.

On the last count, hold this position with the hands clenched at the chest, partners looking sternly at each other for a moment; then shake hands.

Figure 5   Figure 8

REAP THE FLAX

(Swedish)

REAP THE FLAX

(Swedish)

The music consists of two parts of eight measures each.

In fitting the steps and movements to the music, each measure should be counted thus: **"One, two, three."**

The dancers form in parallel ranks of five, all facing in the same direction with hands on hips. [Diag. 1.]

The dancers in each rank are numbered from left to right.

Number One of each rank is its leader (see Diagram 1).

Diagram 1

1. A.

(**Meas. 1.**)   All reach down to the left, as if to seize the flax (**one, two, three**).

(**Meas. 2.**)   Return to standing position and at the same time pull the hands up to the waist as if reaping the flax (**one, two, three**).

(**Meas. 3.**)   Make a movement as if throwing the flax over toward the right side (**one, two, three**).

(**Meas. 4.**)   Hands on hips (**one, two, three**).

(**Meas. 5-8.**)   Repeat the same.

B.

(**Meas. 1-7.**)   All make a quarter-turn to the left so as to be in single files [Diag. 2], Number One

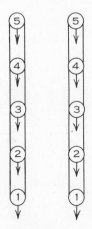

Diagram 2

still keeping hands on hips and each of the others placing hands on the shoulders of the dancer in front, and beginning with the right foot all run around in a circle to the right, making three steps to a measure, and return to place.   (See Diagram 3.)

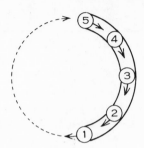

Diagram 3

(**Meas. 8.**)   All placing hands on hips, stamp twice in place and at the same time make a quarter-turn to the right so as to stand in a single rank as before (**one, two**), pause (**three**).

2. A.

(**Meas. 1.**)   All reach down to the right (**one, two, three**).

(**Meas. 2.**)   Return to standing position, as if picking up the flax (**one, two, three**).

(**Meas. 3.**)   Make a movement forward with the arms as if placing the flax around the hackle (**one, two, three**).

(**Meas. 4.**)   Jerk the hands toward the body as if pulling the flax forcibly from the hackle (**one, two, three**).

(**Meas. 5-8.**)   Repeat the same.

B.

Run in a circle as described in **B** of the first figure.

3. A.

Numbers Two and Five step forward out of line and close in so as to form a square with Numbers Three and Four. These four dancers, with the right hands across the centre of the square, grasp the thumbs of the ones at the opposite corners, the left hands still on hips.

These four dancers now represent the spinning-wheel.

Number One, the leader, turns in place and stands facing the other four. The leader now represents the spinner.

(**Meas. 1-4.**)   With twelve running steps, the dancers who form the spinning-wheel run around to the left, making three steps to a measure. [Diag. 4.]

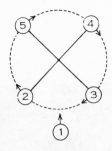

Diagram 4

(**Meas. 5-8.**)   Turn about, grasp left thumbs, and with twelve running steps run around to the right, making three steps to each measure.

During these eight measures, Number One on the first count of each measure beats time with the left foot as if treading the wheel, and at the same time claps hands together to emphasize each beat.

B.

Run in a circle, as described in **B** of first figure.

4. A.

All take the same positions as for **A** of the preceding step.

(**Meas. 1-8.**)   Numbers Two, Three, Four and Five stand still, and Number One, with twenty-four running steps, moves in and out of the square (as shown in Diagram 5): returning to original position.   This figure represents the weaving of the linen, Number One taking the part of the shuttle.

B.

Same as **B** of the first figure.

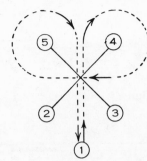

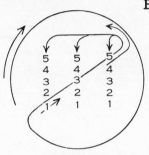

Diagram 5

5. A.

(**Meas. 1-4.**)   With twelve running steps, all the groups of five form into one big circle, joining hands and dancing around to the left.

(**Meas. 5-8.**)   Repeat, dancing around to the right with twelve running steps.

B.

(**Meas. 1-8.**)   All face to the left and, without pausing, the leader of the first group puts hands on hips and all the dancers put their hands on the shoulders in front of them. In this formation, the leader takes them all once around the circle, then diagonally across the centre of the circle (as shown in Diagram 6).

Each group then returns to its original position.

Diagram 6

NOTE.   If there are many dancers, it will be necessary to play the music over until all have had time to return to place.   If they reach their places too soon, the dancers run in place and finish with a quarter-turn to the right on two final stamps (**one, two**), pause (**three**) in the last measure.

KULL-DANSEN—"Lassie Dance"
(Swedish)

Come, will you dance? O yes, I will! Then we will dance, my pret - ty

las - sie! Come, will you dance? O yes, I will! Then we will dance, my pret - ty

las - sie! Las - sie, las - sie, las - sie, las - sie, las - sie, lass,

las - sie, las - sie, las - sie, las - sie, las - sie, lass, Come dance, my pret - ty las - sie!

KULL-DANSEN (Lassie Dance)

(Swedish)

The music consists of two parts, **A** of eight measures and **B** of six measures.

The dancers form in couples in a single circle, all facing the centre. In each couple, Number One is on the left, Number Two on the right. The couples are also numbered from left to right around the circle.

In fitting the steps to the music, each measure is counted thus: "**One, two, three.**"

Figure 1

1. A.

(**Meas. 1.**) With hands on hips, Number One makes a quarter-turn to the left and Number Two makes a quarter-turn to the right, so that they are back to back, and both at the same time place the right foot back with the weight upon it (**one**), both bend the right knee and bow (**two, three**).

(**Meas. 2.**) Both turn about to the right, at the same time transferring the weight to the left foot (**one**), and bow to partner (**two, three**). [Fig. 1.]

(**Meas. 3.**) Both turn about to the left, at the same time transferring weight to the right foot (**one**), and bow (**two, three**).

(**Meas. 4.**) The same as in Meas. 2.

(**Meas. 5-8.**) Repeat the same.

B.

(**Meas. 1-4.**) Partners, facing each other, with a little spring place the weight on the right foot, kicking forward with the left foot, keeping the left knee extended (**one**). Continue, making twelve kicking steps in all, three to each measure, with the right and left feet alternately.

(**Meas. 5-6.**) Numbers One and Two both clap own hands and stamp with the left foot on the first count of Meas. 5, and joining both hands turn each other once around with walking steps, making three steps to a measure; finish facing each other as before.

2. A.

(**Meas. 1.**) Numbers One and Two, with left hands on hips, join right hands and with left knee extended place left foot forward with the toes raised from the floor. Both turn slightly to the right (**one**), pause (**two, three**). [Fig. 2.]

(**Meas. 2.**)   With a spring, change positions of the feet and at the same time change positions of the hands.

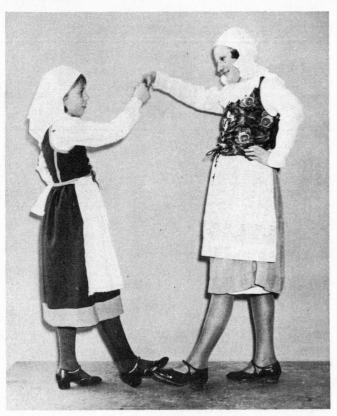

Figure 2

(**Meas. 3-4.**)   The same as in Meas. 1 and 2.
(**Meas. 5-8.**)   Repeat the same.

B.

Same as **B** in the first figure.

At the end of **B,** each odd couple finish by placing themselves inside the circle, with backs to centre of circle and facing the even couple who were at their left, thus forming a square with them.

3. A.

(**Meas. 1-8.**)   All four, with left hands on hips, join right hands across the centre of the square with those at opposite corner of square, and repeat the steps described in **2 A.**

B.

Same as **B** of the first figure.

(At the end of **B,** all finish in their original positions.)

4. A.

Number One stands behind Number Two and places hands on partner's waist. Number Two puts hands on hips.

(**Meas. 1.**)   Number One with left knee extended places the left foot to the side with the toes raised from the floor.   At the same time Number Two, with the right knee extended, places the right foot to the side with toes raised.   Both look around to

Figure 3

the right at each other (**one**), pause in this position (**two**) [Fig. 3], both replace feet which were placed to the side, so that heels are together (**three**).

(**Meas. 2.**)   Both repeat the same movement; but this time with the opposite feet, and both look around to the left at each other.

(**Meas. 3.**)   Same as first measure.

(**Meas. 4.**)   Same as second measure.

(**Meas. 5-8.**)   Repeat the same.

B.

Same as **B** of the first figure.

At the end of **B,** each odd couple forms a square with the even couple next to them, as in Figure 3, but with hands joined so as to form a circle.

5. A.

(**Meas. 1.**)   Stamp forward on the left foot (**one**), draw the right foot up to the left and immediately raise the left foot forward with the knee extended (**two**), hop on the right foot and at the same time bend left knee and bring left foot close to right knee (**three**).

(**Meas. 2-8.**) Continue this step, all four dancing around the circle to the left.

B.

As described in **B** of first figure.
The words are as follows:

A.

Come, will you dance? O yes, I will!
  Then we will dance, my pretty lassie!
Come, will you dance? O yes, I will!
  Then we will dance, my pretty lassie!

B.

Lassie, lassie, lassie, lassie, lassie, lass,
Lassie, lassie, lassie, lassie, lassie, lass,
  Come dance, my pretty lassie!

FJÄLLNÄSPOLSKA

(Mountain Polka)

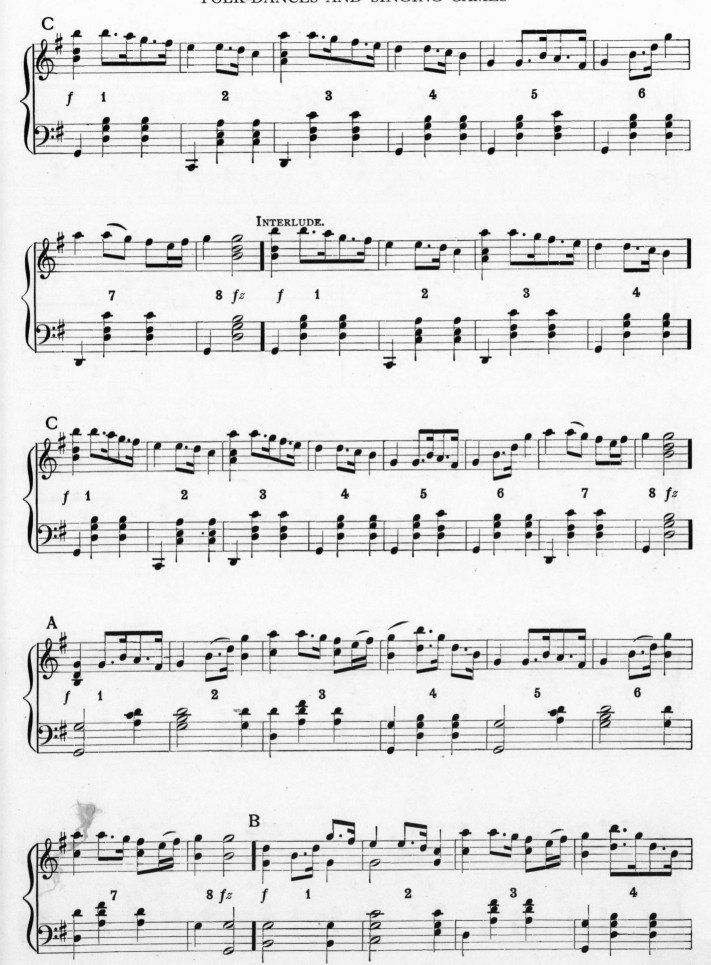

FJÄLLNÄSPOLSKA

(Swedish)

The music has three parts of eight measures each, and an interlude of four measures which is introduced before the repeat of **A**, during the first figure, and again after **C**, during the second figure.

In fitting the steps to the music, each measure should be counted thus: **"One, two, three."** The dancers form in two parallel lines of couples, facing each other. In each couple, the man stands on the left of the girl, and partners join inside hands, placing outside hands on hips.

1. A.

(**Meas. 1.**) Beginning with the right foot, partners run forward three steps toward opposite couples (**one, two, three**).

(**Meas. 2.**) Jump on both feet in place, landing with the feet slightly separated (**one**), pause (**two**), jump the feet together (**three**).

(**Meas. 3.**) Stamp the right foot to the side (**one**), swing the left foot across in front of the right (**two**), hop on the right foot (**three**).

(**Meas. 4.**) Stamp the left foot to the side (**one**), swing the right foot across in front of the left (**two**), hop on the left foot (**three**).

(**Meas. 5.**) Run forward again as in Meas. 1.

(**Meas. 6.**) Same as second measure.

(**Meas. 7.**) Stamp left foot to side (**one**), swing right foot across in front of left (**two**), hop on left (**three**).

(**Meas. 8.**) Stamp the right foot to the side (**one**), swing the left foot across in front of the right (**two**), hop on the right foot (**three**).

INTERLUDE

(**Four Measures.**) Partners face each other, joining right hands, place left hands on hips, and beginning with the left foot continue the same step as in Meas. 7 and 8 preceding.

A. (Repeated.)

(**Meas. 1.**) With a pull with their right hands and beginning with the left foot, partners with hands on hips run three steps forward past each other in the direction in which they were facing during the interlude, thus coming face to face with a dancer from the next couple (**one, two, three**).

(**Meas. 2.**) Jump on both feet in place, landing with the feet slightly apart, and at the same time with hands clenched fling the arms sideward shoulder-high, thus saluting the dancer from the next couple (**one**), pause (**two**), jump, feet together, at the same time bringing the hands back to the chest with the elbows still raised (**three**).

(**Meas. 3.**) Jump on both feet, and at the same time face about to the right (landing facing partner, with the feet slightly apart), and at the same time fling the arms sideward shoulder-high, thus saluting

partner (**one**), pause (**two**), jump the feet together, at the same time bringing the hands back to the chest with the elbows raised (**three**).

(**Meas. 4.**) Still facing partner, salute again as in the third measure.

(**Meas. 5.**) With hands on hips, and beginning with the right foot, partners run three steps forward past each other.

(**Meas. 6.**) Salute the dancer from the couple on the other side as in the second measure.

(**Meas. 7-8.**) Turn and salute partners as in the third and fourth measures.

B.

(**Eight Measures.**) Partners, with backs turned to opposite line, join inside hands, placing outside hands on hips, and return to original position, with same steps as in **A**, Meas. 1-8. Face about toward opposite line at end of Meas. 8.

2. C.

Partners dance toward the opposite line with the following step:

(**Meas. 1.**) Step forward with the right foot (**one**), touch the left foot across in front of the right foot, and at the same time raise both heels and throw the weight forward on to the left foot (**two**); let the heel of the right foot sink, and at the same time transfer the weight to the right foot (**three**).

(**Meas. 2.**) Repeat same, beginning with left foot.

(**Meas. 3.**) With a spring, throw the weight on to the right foot, and at the same time kick forward with the left foot, keeping the left knee extended (**one**); change the position of the feet, kicking forward with the right foot (**two**), change the position of the feet, kicking forward with the left foot (**three**).

(**Meas. 4.**) Jump on both feet in place and land with the feet slightly apart (**one**), pause (**two**), jump the feet together (**three**).

(**Meas. 5-8.**) Repeat same. (This step should bring the two lines close together facing each other.)

INTERLUDE

(**Meas. 1.**) With hands on hips, partners turn slightly away from each other and at the same time touch heel of inside foot to side, keeping knee extended (**one**), pause (**two**), replace inside foot and at the same time pivot a little farther around in place (**three**).

(**Meas. 2-4.**) Complete an outward about-face, continuing as in the first measure. Finish with the backs turned to the opposite line and with inside hands joined, outside hands on hips.

C. (Repeated.)

(**Meas. 1-8.**) Return to original position with same steps as described in first eight measures of the second figure. At the end of the eight measures partners finish face to face with both hands joined.

3. A.

(**Meas. 1.**)   Partners, each facing toward the right, stamp with right foot (**one**), swing left foot forward (**two**), hop on right foot (**three**).

(**Meas. 2.**)   Repeat with the other foot.

(**Meas. 3-4.**)   Partners, each facing toward the left, repeat same as first and second measures.

(**Meas. 5-6.**)   Same as Meas. 1 and 2.

(**Meas. 7-8.**)   Same as Meas. 3 and 4.

B.

(**Meas. 1.**)   Partners, facing each other with both hands still joined, with a spring, place left feet

Figure 1

forward with toes raised and at same time pull back with right hands (**one**), pause (**two, three**).

(**Meas. 2.**)   With a spring change the position of the feet and pull back with left hands.

(**Meas. 3.**)   With three springs change position of feet three times, pulling each time with the hands.

(**Meas. 4.**)   Spring again, placing right foot forward with toes raised, and at the same time pull back with left hand (**one**), pause (**two, three**).

(**Meas. 5-8.**)   Continue as in Meas. 1-4.

C.

Partners face toward the opposite line, with the left hands on the hips, and dance toward the opposite line with the following step:

(**Meas. 1.**)   Stamp forward with right foot and at same time look across at opposite and shield eyes with right hand (**one**). [Fig. 1.] Swing left foot across in front of right (**two**), hop on right (**three**).

(**Meas. 2.**)   Repeat same, using other foot and hand.

(**Meas. 3-4.**)   Same as the first and second measures. (This should bring the two lines close together facing each other.)

(**Meas. 5-6.**)   The man of each couple grasps the girl of the opposite couple by the waist. The girl places hands on the man's shoulders, and with six running steps they turn each other once around to the right in place.

(**Meas. 7.**)   Push vigorously away from each other on the first count and run three steps backward to original positions.

(**Meas. 8.**)   Jump on both feet in place, landing with feet slightly apart, and at same time throw the arms vigorously sideward, shoulder-high, with fists clenched (**one**), pause (**two**), jump feet together and at the same time place hands on hips (**three**).

C.   (Repeated.)

(**Meas. 1-8.**)   Repeat the same. At end of Meas. 8, the man steps quickly behind his partner, and places hands on her waist.

4. A.

(**Meas. 1.**)   The man touches left foot to side with toes raised from floor, keeping left knee extended; at the same time the girl touches right foot to side with toes raised from floor, keeping right knee extended. Both lean to the right and look around at each other (**one**), pause (**two**), both replace the foot that was touched to the side, so that the heels are together (**three**). [Fig. 2.]

(**Meas. 2.**)   Same as Meas. 1, but each uses the other foot and leans to *left* (**one, two, three**).

(**Meas. 3-6.**)   Continue same as Meas. 1 and 2.

(**Meas. 7-8.**)   The man still holding partner's waist, both with six running steps turn once around in place to the right.

A.   (Repeated.)

(**Meas. 1-8.**)   Repeat the same.

At the end of the last measure, the man releases partner's waist, and partners stand back to back with hands on hips and look across at the opposite couple.

5.   B.

(**Meas. 1.**)   The man touches right heel to side toward the girl of opposite couple, and at the same time beckons to her persuasively with right hand (**one**), pause (**two**), replaces right foot to the left (**three**). The girl executes same movements with the left foot, but keeps both hands on hips, and as the man beckons, shakes her head and looks away indifferently. [Fig. 3.]

Figure 2

(**Meas. 2-6.**) Continue same as Meas. 1.

(**Meas. 7-8.**) With six running steps, both turn once around in place, the man to left, the girl to right. Finish back to back, as before.

B. (Repeated.)

(**Meas. 1-8.**) Repeat the same, but this time the girl beckons, and the man shakes his head and looks away indifferently.

C. & C. (Repeated.)

(**Meas. 1-14.**) Partners facing each other, take waist and shoulder grasp (that is, the man grasps his partner by the waist and she places hands on his shoulders) and all dance "Hambo" around in a large circle which moves in the direction opposite to the hands of the clock, at the same time that the couples revolve in the direction of the hands of the clock.

(**Meas. 15-16.**) The girl makes a spring and at the same time her partner lifts her as high as possible from the ground. This concludes the dance.

As the Hambo is difficult to master from a written description besides being hard to perform without the help of a Swedish partner, a simple modification of the step is suggested here for practical purposes. The description is for the girl, the man's step being the same with the other foot:

(**Meas. 1.**) Step onto the right foot (**one**), make a slight hop on it (**two**), put down the left foot and take the weight off of the right foot (**three**).

(**Meas. 2.**) Repeat the same. Continue in this manner.

While dancing this together the couple revolve and move around the room as described above for the Hambo.

The Fjällnäspolska is not a true folk-dance, being a comparatively modern arrangement of various Swedish folk-dance steps. It has been adopted however, by the Swedish Folk-Dance Society in Sweden, and is one of their favorite dances.

Figure 3

KAMARINSKAIA

(Russian)

Arr. by Emma Howells Burchenal

KAMARINSKAIA

(Russian)

The Russian Kamarinskaia is composed of an almost unlimited number of steps, from which the dancer makes his own selection according to his ability or inclination. Some of these steps call for great strength and agility on the part of the dancer and are usually executed only by a man.

The steps here described have been selected from a large number and simplified so that they may be put to practical use.

The music here given is a combination of two Russian folk-melodies, and consists of three distinct strains of sixteen measures each. In fitting the steps to the music, each measure should be counted thus: **"One, and, two, and."**

The dance is here described as done by two people, Numbers One and Two; but it can be danced by a larger number divided into sections one and two, each in single file behind one of the leaders.

The following steps are described *as executed by Number One;* and it is to be understood that, except when otherwise specified, *Number Two executes the counterpart of these*, that is, he uses the opposite hand or foot and moves in the opposite direction.

I. A.

With the left hand on the hip, right arm extended forward, palm up; right leg extended forward, toes up:

(**Meas. 1.**) Both Number Two and Number One step forward with the right foot, the heel touching the floor (**one**), close the left foot to the right (**and**), step forward with the right foot (**two**), raise the left foot forward, toes up with knee extended (**and**).

(**Meas. 2.**) Repeat same beginning with the left foot and swinging the extended right arm across the body to the left, palm down (**one, and, two, and**).

(**Meas. 3-16.**) Continue the same. Finish (arms folded, elbows shoulder-high) with three stamps in place, left foot (**one**), right foot (**and**), left (**two**), pause (**and**).

In executing this step Numbers One and Two start from opposite corners of the rear of the danc- 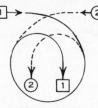 ing space, and move forward and around in a circle, as shown in the diagram. [Diag. 1.] The arm should be swung from side to side vigorously, the head thrown back and turned so that the dancer is looking out from the circle, and the body bent

Diagram 1

from side to side in the direction of the swinging of the arm.

2. B.

(**Meas. 1.**) With arms extended sideways (the right diagonally upward and the left diagonally downward), step to the side with the right foot (**one**), and across behind with the left foot (**and**), step sideward with the right foot (**two**), across behind with the left foot (**and**).

(**Meas. 2-3.**) Continue the same, moving to the right. [Diag. 2.]

Diagram 2

(**Meas. 4.**) Step to the side again with the right foot (**one, and**). Stamp the left foot across in front of the right, and extend both arms diagonally downward to the right.

(**Meas. 5-8.**) Repeat same step in the opposite direction, beginning with the left foot.

(**Meas. 9-12.**) Same as Meas. 1-4.

(**Meas. 13-15.**) Same as Meas. 5-7.

(**Meas. 16.**) Finish with three stamps in place and arms folded (**one, and, two**), pause (**and**).

Execute this step as if running sideward, but without any up and down motion.

3. C.

(**Meas. 1.**) Both Number Two and Number One, with left hand placed back of the neck and right hand at waist, the head turned sharply to the right, looking over the right shoulder, touch the right toe to the side with the foot reversed so that

the heel is uppermost and at the same time hop on the left foot (**one, and**), extend the right foot forward, and at the same time hop on the left foot (**two, and**).

(**Meas. 2.**) Change the position of the hands, and repeat the same with the left foot.

(**Meas. 3-4.**) Continue the same.

(**Meas. 5.**) With arms folded, head inclined to the left, and left foot raised close behind the right knee, put the left foot down close behind the right foot (**one**), raise the right foot back of the left knee and incline the head to right (**and**), put the right foot down close behind the left foot (**two**), raise the left foot behind the right knee and incline the head to the left (**and**).

(**Meas. 6-8.**) Continue the same.

(**Meas. 9-16.**) Repeat the same, this time beginning with the left foot.

This step, during Measures 5-8 and 9-16, is executed on the toes and walking backward with a springy step, and with exaggerated knee-raising before each step. Turn the knee to the side when raising it.

4. A.

On "**and**" of the preceding measure hop on the left foot, with left hand placed back of the neck, right hand at the waist, head turned to the right and right foot raised to the knee.

(**Meas. 1.**) Slide the right foot to the side (**one**), close the left foot to the right (**and**), displacing the right foot which is immediately extended to the side (**two**), raise the right foot behind the left knee and at the same time hop on the left foot (**and**).

(**Meas. 2-3.**) Continue this mazurka-step, moving to the right. [Diag. 2.]

(**Meas. 4.**) With arms folded, finish with three stamps in place; right (**one**), left (**and**), right (**two**), pause (**and**).

(**Meas. 5-8.**) Change the position of the arms and repeat the same, but beginning with the left foot and moving to the left.

(**Meas. 9-12.**) Same as Meas. 1-4.

(**Meas. 13-16.**) Same as Meas. 5-8.

5. B.

Both Number Two and Number One, with left hand back of the neck, and right hand at the waist, touch the right toe to the side in reversed position so that the heel is uppermost, at the same time hop on the left foot (**one, and**), turn the right foot so that the toes are raised, and touch the heel in the same spot, and at the same time hop on the left foot (**two, and**).

(**Meas. 2.**) Touch the right toe in front of the left toe and at the same time hop on the left foot (**one, and**), extend the right foot forward and at the same time hop on the left foot (**two, and**).

(**Meas. 3-4.**) Repeat the same, but with the left foot moving and the right hand back of the neck.

(**Meas. 5-8.**) Walk backward with springy steps as in Meas. 5-8 of **3.**

(**Meas. 9-16.**) Repeat all, this time beginning with the left foot.

In this step the shoulders are turned away from the foot, which is pointing in the reverse position, but the head is turned toward it.

6. C.

On "**and**" of the preceding measure hop on the left foot with arms swung sideways and up slightly above the shoulder-level and the right leg extended and raised sideward.

(**Meas. 1.**) Step to the side with the right foot, and at the same time swing the arms down and across each other and give a short, vigorous shout (**one, and**), step across behind with the left foot, immediately raising the right leg extended to the side and swinging the arms sideways and up (**two**), hop on the left foot (**and**).

(**Meas. 2-3.**) Continue the same, moving to the right. [Diag. 2.]

(**Meas. 4.**) Step to the side again with the right foot, swinging the arms down and across each other as before (**one, and**), close the left foot to the right at the same time swinging the arms sideward and up as before (**two**).

(**Meas. 5-8.**) Repeat the same, beginning with the left foot and moving to the left.

(**Meas. 9-15.**) Same as Meas. 1-7.

(**Meas. 16.**) With arms folded, make three stamps in place.

In executing this step, move sideward, even in hopping. In swinging the arms down, bend the body forward; and when the arms are swung up, throw back the head and look in the direction of the step. Cover as much distance as possible, moving fiercely as if impatient at not being able to cover more distance.

7. A.

(**Meas. 1.**) With arms crossed diagonally downward, bend the knees and sit on the heels (**one, and**); extend the knees, springing to astride position standing on the heels with the toes raised. At the same time swing the arms sideward and up to shoulder-level (**two, and**).

(**Meas. 2-4.**) Continue the same.

While executing this step, move forward gradually.

(**Meas. 5-8.**) Walk backward with springy steps as in Meas. 5-8 of **3.**

(**Meas. 9-15.**) Same as Meas. 1-7.

(**Meas. 16.**) Three stamps in place.

8. A.

(**Meas. 1.**) With arms folded, slide the left foot diagonally forward to the left, the right leg extended

backward and raised (**one, and**); in this position hop on the left foot (**two, and**). [Diag. 3.]

Diagram 3

(**Meas. 2.**) Beginning with the right foot, stamp three times, at the same time turning once around to the left in place.

(**Meas. 3.**) With the arms still folded, slide the right foot diagonally forward to the right, the left leg extended backward and raised (**one, and**). In this position, hop on right foot (**two, and**). [Diag. 4.]

Diagram 4

(**Meas. 4.**) Beginning with the left foot, stamp three times, turning once and a quarter around to the right in place. Number Two uses the opposite foot, so that the partners slide first away from each other and turn outward, then slide toward each other and turn inward. Finish facing partner, and on the last stamp both Number One and Number Two extend the left arm diagonally upward to the side and the right arm out to the side shoulder-high with the palm up.

(**Meas. 5.**) Standing side by side, facing in opposite directions, with right arm placed around partner's waist in front, both step forward with the left foot (**one, and**), step forward with the right foot (**two**), hop on the right foot (**and**).

(**Meas. 6-7.**) Continue the same, at the same time swinging partner in place.

(**Meas. 8.**) Finish with three stamps and, Number Two releasing partner's waist, both face toward the front, standing side by side; Number Two with right arm extended sideward shoulder-high, left arm still raised diagonally upward to the side; Number One with right arm still around partner's waist, left arm diagonally upward (**one, and, two**), pause in this position (**and**).

(**Meas. 9-16.**) Same as Meas. 1-8; and finish with a vigorous shout given at the instant of the final stamp.

In the turn, both use the same hands and feet, each helping the other with the right arm so that the swing is a vigorous one.

HIGHLAND FLING

(Scottish)

Arr. by EMMA HOWELLS BURCHENAL

* Play A once for introduction, then begin and play entire dance five times.

HIGHLAND FLING
(Scottish)

The music is in two parts, **A** and **B**, of 8 measures each. In fitting steps to music, count thus: (1st measure) "one, two"; (2d measure) "three, four."

INTRODUCTION.
A.

(**Meas. 1-6.**) With arms akimbo and hands turned so that knuckles rest on the hips, stand still with heels together until the last count of the sixth measure, when the dancer springs off of both feet, spreading the feet apart (with knees straight) while in the air [Fig. 1]. (**Meas. 7.**) On first note

Fig. 1.

of measure, land on both feet with left foot in third position in front (**one**); pause (**and, two**); spring again, spreading the feet while in the air (**and**).

(**Meas. 8.**) On first note of measure, land on both feet, with right foot in third position in front (**three**); pause (**and, four**), and go right into the

First Step.—"simple fling."
A.

(**Meas. 1-2.**) With left arm raised overhead (the wrist slightly bent and thumb touching the second finger) make a little spring and land on the toes with feet slightly apart (**one**) [Fig. 2]; hop on left foot and at same time bring up right foot close to and behind left calf, keeping right knee turned out directly to the side (**two**). Hop on left foot again,

and at the same time bring right foot with the smallest possible movement around in front of and close

Fig. 2.

to left leg at same height as before (**three**) [Fig. 3]; hop again on left foot, and bring right foot around behind again (**four**).

(**Meas. 3-4.**) Repeat the same, with the opposite foot and arm. (**Meas. 5-6.**) Same as meas. 1-2.

(**Meas. 7-8.**) Same as meas. 1-2, but at the same time turn once around to the right in place, with both hands on hips [Fig. 4].

B.

(**Meas. 1-8.**) Repeat the whole step, beginning with the left foot and right arm.

Second Step.
A.

(**Meas. 1.**) Like meas. 1 of first step (**one, two**).

(**Meas. 2.**) Hop on left foot; at same time touch right toe diagonally forward (**three**); hop again on left foot, and at same time bring right foot close in front of left leg at same height as before (**four**).

(**Meas. 3-4.**) With both hands on hips, turn once around to right as in meas. 7-8 of first step.

(**Meas. 5-8.**) Repeat all beginning with a hop on right foot, right arm raised, turning to the left.

B.

(**Meas. 1-8.**) Repeat the whole step again.

Third Step.—"BACK FOOTING."

A.

(**Meas. 1.**) Same as meas. 1 of first step (**one, two**). (**Meas. 2.**) Hop on left foot, and at same time touch right toe diagonally forward (**three**); hop again

Fig. 3.

on left foot, and at same time bring right foot close in front of left leg at same height as before (**four**).

(**Meas. 3-4.**) With both hands on hips, and beginning with right foot, make four "back footing" steps in place. These "back footing" steps are four running steps in place, done thus : starting with right foot raised behind left knee, with right knee sharply bent and turned out to side, put down right foot behind and under left foot, at same time lifting left foot behind right knee, with left knee sharply bent and turned out to side (**one**); put down left foot in same way (**two**); continue (**three, four**).

(**Meas. 5-8.**) Repeat, as in Meas. 1-4, beginning with left foot.

B.

(**Meas. 1-8.**) Repeat the whole step.

Fourth Step.—"SIDE" STEP.

A.

(**Meas. 1-2**). Same as meas. 1-2 of first step. (**Meas. 3-4.**) With left arm still raised, spring, and land on the toes with feet apart, bearing more weight on left foot than on right (**one**); pause (**two**). Hop sidewise to left on left foot, and at same time bring

right foot raised close in front of left ankle (**and**); put down right foot across in front of left foot (**three**); spring off both feet, separating them while in the air (**and**); land on both feet with left in third position in front (**four**). Accent the preceding four counts thus: "**One, two, three, four.**"

(**Meas. 5-8.**) Repeat the same, beginning with the left foot, and moving to the right.

B.

(**Meas. 1-8.**) Repeat the whole step again.

Fifth Step.—"ROCKING" STEP.

A.

(**Meas. 1-2.**) Same as meas. 1-2 of first step (**one, two**). With left arm still raised, hop on left foot and at same time touch right toe a little to right of the left toe (**three**) [Fig. 5]; hop again on left foot and extend right foot diagonally forward, extending knee with a little shake (**four**) [Fig. 6].

Fig. 4.

(**Meas. 3-4.**) With both hands on hips, "rock" four times. These "rocking" steps are done thus : Bring right toe close to and a little to the right of left toe, and immediately put down right foot, at same time raising left foot, so that only tip of toe touches the floor (**one**); put down left foot, at same time raising right foot, so that only tip of toe touches the floor (**two**). Continue same (**three, four**).

(**Meas. 5-8.**) Repeat same, beginning with left foot.

B.

(**Meas. 1-8.**) Repeat the whole step.

Sixth Step.—"FRONT FOOTING."

A.

(**Meas. 1.**) Same as meas. 1 of first step (**one, two**.) (**Meas. 2.**) With both hands on hips, make

Fig. 5.

same time bring the right foot around and touch it close in front of the left leg at the usual height

Fig. 6.

(**three**); strike right foot again in the same place, at the same time hopping again on left foot (**four**).

two "front footing" steps, beginning with right foot (**three, four**). "Front footing" is done exactly like the "back footing" already described, except that the foot is put down in front of instead of behind the other [Fig. 7]. (**Meas. 3-4.**) With left arm raised, hop on left foot, and at same time touch right foot diagonally forward (**one**); hop on left foot again and at same time bring right foot close in front of left leg at the usual height (**two**). Repeat the same (**three, four**). (**Meas. 5-6.**) With both hands on hips and beginning with right foot, make four "back footing" steps (**one, two, three, four**). (**Meas. 7-8.**) With hands still on hips, turn once around to right, as in meas. 7-8 of the first step.

B.

(**Meas. 1-8.**) Repeat the same, beginning with the left foot and right arm.

Seventh Step.

A.

(**Meas. 1.**) Same as meas. 1 of first step (**one, two**). (**Meas. 2.**) Hop on the left foot, and at the

Fig. 7.

(**Meas. 3-4.**) With both hands on hips, hop on left foot, and at same time touch right foot diagonally

Fig. 8.

forward (**one**); hop again on left foot, and at same time bring right foot close in front of left leg at the usual height (**two**). Put right foot down in front, at same time raising left foot close to and behind right calf (**three**); hop on right foot and at same time bring left foot around close to and in front of right leg at the usual height (**four**).

(**Meas. 5-8.**) Repeat the same, beginning with the left foot and right arm.

B.

(**Meas. 1-8.**) Repeat the whole step.

Eighth Step.— "TOE AND HEEL."

A.

(**Meas. 1-2.**) Same as meas. 1-2 of first step.

(**Meas. 3-4.**) With both hands on hips, hop on the left foot, and at the same time touch the right toe close to and a little to the right of the left toe (**one**) [Fig. 8]; hop again on the left foot and touch the right heel in the same place (**two**) [Fig. 9]. "Toe and heel" with the left foot in the same manner (**three, four**). (**Meas. 5-6.**) Same as meas. 3-4.

(**Meas. 7-8.**) With hands still on hips, turn once around to the right as in meas. 7-8 of first step.

B.

(**Meas. 1-8.**) Repeat the step, beginning with the left foot and right arm.

Ninth Step.—"THE FINISH."

A.

(**Meas. 1-2.**) Same as meas. 1-2 of first step.

Fig. 9.

(**Meas. 3.**) Like meas. 1 of first step (**one, two**).

(**Meas. 4.**) With left arm still raised, hop on left foot, and at the same time touch right foot diagonally forward (**three**); hop again on the left foot, and at the same time bring the right foot close to and in front of the left leg at the usual height (**four**).

(**Meas. 5-6.**) With both hands on hips, turn around to the right in place, as in meas. 7-8 of first step. (**Meas. 7-8.**) Without stopping, turn around still another time to the right as in meas. 5-6.

B.

(**Meas. 1-8.**) Repeat the whole, beginning with left foot and right arm. On last note stop, and hold for a moment the final position of right foot close to and behind left calf, with both hands on hips.

Throughout dance, movements of feet should be small and exact, and made from the knee, without rotating the thigh, and with toes carefully pointed. The knees should always be turned out directly toward the side. Observe this rule strictly, especially whenever the knee of the free foot is bent.

In changing hands from hips to overhead, and vice versa, they should pass each other in front of body. When hands are placed on hips, turn them so as to rest knuckles down, with wrists straight.

FOURSOME REEL

(Scotch)

Arr. by EMMA HOWELLS BURCHENAL
Play 8 measures as Introduction

FOURSOME REEL

(Scottish)

The reel has two distinct parts, the slow and the quick. The music for the slow part is a Strathspey (Highland Fling time) of sixteen measures (**A**), while the quick part is a Reel (quick time) of sixteen measures (**B**). The Strathspey is repeated again and again throughout the slow time, and then, without any pause between, the Reel is begun, and played until the conclusion of the dance.

Music for the Scottish dances should properly be played upon the bagpipes, as no other instrument can express the peculiar quality and rhythm of the Scottish dance-music (see Fig. 1).

Figure 1

In fitting the steps to the Strathspey music it should be counted thus: (First measure) **"one, two"**; (second measure) **"three, four."** In the Reel time each measure should be counted thus: **"One, and, two, and."**

FORMATION

The dancers, four in number, stand about four feet apart in a single line. The two at either end of the line are partners and stand facing each other; this brings the two middle ones back to back. When girls and men are dancing together, the men are in the middle and the girls are at either end.

THE STEPS

The steps used during the dance are Highland Fling steps, Reel steps, the "walk around" in Highland Fling time, and the "walk around" in Reel time. The "walk around" step in both cases is the simple *schottische* or "Scottish" step, as follows: Step forward with the right foot (**one**), close the left foot to the right foot (**two**), step forward with the right foot (**three**), hop on the right foot and at the same time extend the left foot forward (**four**).

In dancing it in Reel time it is done much more quickly than in Highland Fling time.

During the "walk around" both arms are curved and raised forward, so that the hands are about at head level, and a little further apart than the width of the shoulders [Fig. 2]. When the step is taken with the right foot, the right shoulder should be turned slightly to the front, and vice versa.

Figure 2

THE DANCE

INTRODUCTION

A.

(**Meas. 1-8.**) The four dancers stand still in the formation already described, with hands on hips (knuckles down) and heels together [Fig. 3].

SLOW PART (Strathspey)

"Walk Around"

1. A.

(**Meas. 1-16.**) All "walk around," describing a figure as indicated in Diagram A. In doing this

Figure 3

use the "Scottish" step, beginning with the right foot and starting forward and toward the left. The girls go all the way round the figure, returning to original position. The men, however, do not quite complete the full figure, but finish in exchanged positions. [Diagrams B and C.]

Diagram A

(**Meas. 1-16.**) Facing new partners, all dance the step described as the first step of the Highland Fling.

First Man

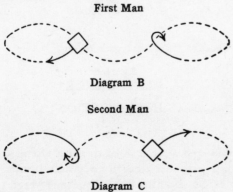

Diagram B

Second Man

Diagram C

2. A.

(**Meas. 1-16.**) All "walk around" as before, the men exchanging positions again, thus returning to original partners.

(**Meas. 1-16.**) All dance any one of the Highland Fling steps.

3. A.

(**Meas. 1-16.**) All "walk around" as in 1.

(**Meas. 1-16.**) All dance another Highland Fling step, and at the finish, without any pause between, the quick part of the dance begins.

QUICK PART (Reel)

1. B.

(**Meas. 1-8.**) All "walk around" as before, but in quick time. (It is necessary to cover ground rapidly in order to complete the figure in eight measures of the music.)

First Reel Step

(**Meas. 9.**) With hands on hips (knuckles down), spring to the right onto the right foot (**one**), touch the left toe close to the right toe (on the inside) and at the same time rise on the toe (**and**); lower the right heel with the weight on the right foot (**two, and**).

(**Meas. 10.**) Repeat the same to the left.

(**Meas. 11.**) With the arms raised as in the "walk around," spring onto the right foot; at the same time touch the tip of the left toe close to the right toe (on the inside) (**one, and**); spring onto the left toe and at the same time touch the tip of the right toe close to the left toe (on the inside) (**two, and**) [Fig. 4].

Figure 4

(**Meas. 12.**)   Continue same as Meas. 11.

(**Meas. 13-16.**)   Same as Meas. 9-12.

2. B.

(**Meas. 1-8.**)   All "walk around" as before.

Second Reel Step

(**Meas. 9.**)   Hop on the left foot and at the same time touch the right toe close to the left toe (on the inside) (**one, and**); hop on the left foot and at the same time straighten the right knee and extend the right foot diagonally forward (**two**); make a slight hop on the left foot (**and**) [Fig. 5].

Figure 5

(**Meas. 10.**)   Swing the right foot around and put it down across behind the left foot (**one**); make a short step to the left with the left foot (**and**); make a short step across in front of the left foot with the right foot (**two**); pause (**and**).

(**Meas. 11-12.**)   Repeat the same as in Meas. 9-10, but beginning with a hop on the right foot [Fig. 6].

(**Meas. 13-14.**)   Same as Meas. 9-10.

(**Meas. 15-16.**)   With arms raised as in the "walk around" make four "toe touchings" as described in Meas. 11-12 of the first "reel" step.

3. B.

(**Meas. 1-8.**)   All "walk around" as before.

Third Reel Step

(**Meas. 9.**)   Put down the right foot, with the toe turned well out, in front of the left foot and at the same time raise the left foot slightly just behind the right heel (**one, and**); put down the left foot and at the same time raise the right foot slightly just in front of the left toe (**two, and**). (This is called "rocking," and in executing it the knees should be turned well out to the side.)

(**Meas. 10.**)   Hop twice on the left foot, at the same time extending the right knee and swinging the right foot forward, sidewise, and around behind the left foot (**one, and**). Put the right foot down behind the left foot (**two**); pause (**and**).

(**Meas. 11-12.**)   Repeat the same as Meas. 9-10, but with the left foot.

(**Meas. 13-14.**)   Repeat the same as in Meas. 9-10, but with the right foot.

(**Meas. 15-16.**)   Finish with four "toe touchings," as at the finish of the preceding "reel" step, and hold for a moment the final attitude: the arms raised, and the right toe touched close to and inside the left toe.

Figure 6

CSÁRDÁS
(Hungarian)

ČZÁRDÁS—No. 1

(Hungarian)

The Čzárdás here described is the one that is danced most commonly by Hungarians both in the ballroom and in the country.

It is danced in couples.

The music consists of two sections of eight measures each, which are repeated indefinitely according to the length of the dance.

In fitting the steps to the music, each measure should be counted thus: **"One, and, two, and, three, and, four, and."**

The dancers stand in couples facing each other, Number One, the man, with hands on partner's waist, Number Two, the girl, with hands on partner's shoulders; or sometimes partners simply join both hands.

A.

(**Meas. 1.**) Number One stamps to the side with the left foot (**one, and**), closes the right foot to the left, striking the heels sharply together (**two, and**), stamps to the side with the right foot (**three, and**), closes the left foot to the right, striking the heels together (**four, and**).

(**Meas. 2-8.**) Continue the same step.

Number Two executes same step, beginning with right foot, so that both step in the same direction each time.

B.

(**Meas. 1-4.**) Beginning with the left foot, partners turn each other around to the right in place, making four walking steps to a measure; and on **"three, and, four, and"** of the fourth measure, close the right foot to the left, striking the heels together (**three, and**), pause (**four, and**).

(**Meas. 5-8.**) Beginning with the right foot, make the same walking turn in the other direction, finishing with the same striking of the heels (**three, and**), pause (**four, and**) in the eighth measure.

C (Music of A).

(**Meas. 1.**) Number One touches the left toe to the side with the position of the foot reversed, so that the heel is uppermost, and at the same time hops on the right foot (**one, and**). turns the foot so that the toes are raised and touches the heel in the same spot, at the same time hopping on the right foot (**two, and**); hop on the left foot and at the same time touch the right toe to the side with the position of the foot reversed so that the heel is uppermost (**three, and**), turn the foot so that the toes are raised and touch the heel in the same spot, at the same time hopping on the left foot (**four, and**).

(**Meas. 2-8.**) Continue the same step.

Simultaneously Number Two executes the same step, beginning with the *right* foot.

D (Music of B).

Partners turn each other in place with following step:

(**Meas. 1.**) Step forward on the left foot, each partner facing obliquely to his left (**one, and**) step forward with the right foot (**two**), hop on the right foot (**and**), step forward on the left foot (**three, and**), step forward with the right foot (**four**), hop on the right foot (**and**).

(**Meas 2-3.**) Continue the same step.

(**Meas. 4.**) Step forward on the left foot (**one, and**), step forward with the right foot (**two**), hop on the right foot (**and**), step forward with left foot (**three, and**), with a jump bring the heels together with a sharp crack and face squarely toward partner (**four**), pause (**and**).

(**Meas. 5-8.**) Repeat the same step, beginning with the right foot and turning in the opposite direction.

During this step the partners should lean the weight away from each other, and swing each other vigorously.

These steps may be continued indefinitely, according to the inclination of the dancers.

ČZÁRDÁS—No. 2

(Hungarian)

The more difficult Čzárdás steps are often danced as a solo by expert Hungarian dancers, and the following is an arrangement of some of the most characteristic steps. When danced in this way, it is called a "Hungarian Solo."

The music given for Čzárdás Number One is

also suitable for this dance, and each measure is counted in the same way.

1. A.

(**Meas. 1.**) With arms folded, elbows raised to shoulder-level, touch the right toe to the side with the position of the foot reversed so that heel is uppermost and at the same time hop on the left foot (**one, and**), turn the foot so that the toes are raised, and touch the heel in the same spot, at the same time hop on the left foot (**two, and**). Hop on the right foot and at the same time touch the left toe to the side with the position of the foot reversed so that the heel is uppermost (**three, and**), turn the foot so that the toes are raised, and touch the heel on the same spot; at the same time hop on the right foot (**four, and**).

(**Meas. 2-7.**) Continue the same step.

(**Meas. 8.**) Hop on the left foot, and at the same time touch the right toe directly in front of the left (**one, and**), exchange the positions of the feet (**two, and**), exchange the positions of the feet again (**three, and**), pause in this position (**four, and**).

2. B.

(**Meas. 1.**) Slide the right foot to the side (**one, and**), bring the left foot to the right, immediately throwing the weight on the left foot, and raise the right leg extended to the side (**two**); bring the right foot to the left (**and**), slide the left foot to the side (**three, and**), bring the right foot to the left, immediately raising the left leg extended to the side (**four**), bring the left foot to the right (**and**).

(**Meas. 2-7.**) Continue the same step.

(**Meas. 8.**) Finish as described for Meas. 8 of 1 A.

3. B.

(**Meas. 1.**) With right hand at the waist and left arm curved diagonally upward, touch the right toe straight to the side in reversed position so that the heel is uppermost, and at the same time hop on the left foot (**one, and**); turn the foot so that the toes are raised, and touch the heel in the same spot, at the same time hop on the left foot (**two, and**); touch the right toe directly in front of the left toe and at the same time hop on the left foot (**three, and**); extend the right foot diagonally forward and at the same time hop on the left foot (**four, and**).

(**Meas. 2.**) With the position of the arms reversed, hop on the right foot and at the same time touch the left toe to the side with the foot in reversed position so that the heel is uppermost (**one, and**); turn the foot so that the toes are raised, and touch

the heel in the same spot, at the same time hop on the right foot (**two, and**); touch the left toe directly in front of the right toe, and at the same time hop on the right foot (**three, and**); extend the left foot diagonally forward, at the same time hop on the right foot (**four, and**).

(**Meas. 3-7.**) Continue the same step.

(**Meas. 8.**) Finish as described for Meas. 8 of 1 A.

4. B.

(**Meas. 1.**) With arms folded, slide to the side with the right foot (**one, and**), bring the left foot to the right, immediately throwing the weight on it and raising right leg extended to the side (**two**), raise the right foot to the left knee, and at the same time hop on the left foot (**and**), slide to the side with the right foot (**three, and**); bring the left foot to the right, instantly throwing the weight on it and raising the right leg extended to the side (**four**); bring the right foot to the left knee, at the same time hopping on the left foot (**and**).

(**Meas. 2.**) Hop on the right foot and at the same time touch the left toe directly in front of the right toe (**one, and**); exchange the positions of the feet (**two, and**); exchange the positions of the feet again (**three, and**); pause (**four**); raise the left foot to the right knee and at the same time hop on the right foot (**and**).

(**Meas. 3.**) Same step as first measure, but using the left foot and moving to the left.

(**Meas. 4.**) Same as second measure, but beginning with the other foot.

(**Meas. 5-8.**) Repeat all.

5. A.

(**Meas. 1.**) Stamp the right foot (**one**), stamp the left foot (**and**), stamp the right foot (**two**), pause (**and**); repeat (**three, and, four, and**).

While making these six stamps, turn once around to the right in place.

(**Meas. 2.**) Hop on the right foot, and at the same time touch the left toe directly in front of the right toe (**one, and**), exchange the positions of the feet (**two, and**); exchange positions of the feet again (**three, and**), pause (**four, and**).

(**Meas. 3.**) Same as first measure, but begin with the left foot and turn around to the left.

(**Meas. 4.**) Same as second measure, but begin with the other foot.

(**Meas. 5-8.**) Repeat all.

The turns in this step are done with the face toward the front as much as possible; looking back over the left shoulder at the beginning of the turn, and turning the head quickly over the other shoulder in the second half of the turn. The stamps are vigorous and snappy.

6. B.

(**Meas. 1.**) Beginning with the right foot raised to the side, hop on the left foot and at the same time strike the right heel sharply against the left heel (**one, and**); hop again on the left foot and at the same time strike the right heel against the left heel (**two, and**). (In making these two hops, move to the right, covering as much distance as possible.) Make a long step sideward with the right foot (**three, and**), with the left foot step across behind the right foot (**four, and**).

(**Meas. 2.**) Same as first measure.

(**Meas 3.**) Touch the right toe to the side, with the foot turned so that the heel is uppermost, at the same time hop on the left foot (**one, and**); turn the right foot and touch the heel in the same spot and at the same time hop on the left foot (**two, and**); hop on the right foot, and at the same time touch the left toe to the side with the heel uppermost (**three, and**); turn the left foot, and touch the heel in the same spot (**four, and**).

(**Meas. 4.**) Hop on the right foot, and at the same time touch the left toe directly in front of the right toe (**one, and**); exchange the positions of the feet (**two, and**), exchange the positions of the feet again (**three, and**), pause (**four, and**).

(**Meas. 5-8.**) Repeat all, beginning with the other foot and moving toward the left.

7. A.

(**Meas. 1-8.**) Same as the fifth step, but this time the music is played very rapidly and the turns are made correspondingly fast. The whole dance should have military dash and precision. The head should be held up and back; the elbows, when the arms are folded, should be kept shoulder-high.

ONE, TWO, THREE, FOUR AND FIVE (Stigare)
(Finnish)

ONE, TWO, THREE, FOUR and FIVE

(Stigare)
(Finnish)

Any number of couples form a single line, or a single circle around the room, with each girl on the right of her partner. Partners then face each other and take waist and shoulder dancing position, that is, the boy places a hand on either side of the girl's waist while she places her hands on his shoulders.

A.

(**Meas. 1-2.**) Couples dance three side-steps moving directly to the side, or toward the center of the circle, the girls starting with right feet and moving to their right and the boys starting with left feet and moving to their left. [Diag. 1.] The three side-steps, for the girls, are as follows: step to the right with the right foot (**one**), close the left foot to the right (**and**), step again to the right with the right foot (**two**), close the left foot to the right (**and**), step again to the right with the right foot (**three**), close the left foot to the right (**and**), stamp in place with the right foot (**four**), pause in this position (**and**). The boys dance this in the same manner but starting with the left foot.

(**Meas. 3-4.**) Repeat the same, retracing foot-steps in the opposite direction, beginning with the other foot and moving away from the center of the circle.

B.

(**Meas. 5.**) Make one step to the side toward the center of the circle, with the foot on that side (**one**), close the other foot to it (**and**), stamp in place with the foot on the side nearest the center (**two**), pause in this position (**and**).

(**Meas. 6.**) Repeat the same in the opposite direction (**three, and, four, and**).

(**Meas. 7-8.**) Keeping the same grasp, partners swing once around in place with four hop-steps, turning in the direction of the hands of the clock. The hop-step for the girl is as follows: step on the right foot (**one**), and hop on that foot (**and**), step on the left foot (**two**), and hop on that foot (**and**), and continue in this manner. The boy dances in the same manner beginning with the left foot.

(**Meas. 5-8.**) Repeat B. as before.

Repeat the whole dance from the beginning and continue in this manner.

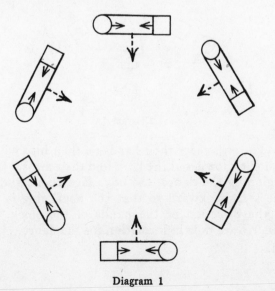

Diagram 1

OLD ONE FROM LAUKA (Vanha Laukaalainen)

(Finnish)

OLD ONE FROM LAUKA
(Vanha Laukaalainen)

(Finnish)

An even number of couples, standing one behind the other, form a circle facing in the direction opposite to the hands of the clock, with each girl on the right of her partner. In this way a double circle is formed with the boys inside and the girls outside. [Diag. 1.]

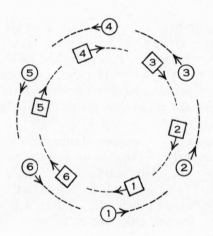

Diagram 2

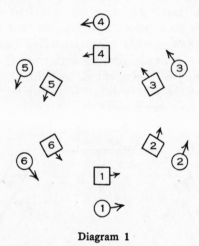

Diagram 1

The girls place their hands on their hips with the knuckles down and the boys fold their arms. Before beginning the dance, the boys face about and take one step backward so that the boys' ring is faced in the direction of the hands of the clock. The dancers are now in formation for the dance. [Diag. 2.]

A.

(**Meas. 1-2.**) Beginning with the right foot, all walk three steps forward in the direction in which they are facing, partners passing each other left shoulder to left shoulder [Fig. 1] and on the fourth count bring the feet together closing the left foot to the right.

(**Meas. 3-4.**) All about face to the left and retrace their footsteps in the opposite direction, partners passing each other right shoulder to right shoulder, and bring their feet together on the fourth count as before.

(**Meas. 1-4.**) Repeat the same.

Figure 1

B.

(**Meas. 5-8.**) Partners join both hands and swing around in place with eight walking steps, turning in the direction of the hands of the clock.

(**Meas. 5-8.**) Then swing around in the same manner in the opposite direction, and at the finish of the swing each dancer takes one step forward so as to progress to a new partner.

Repeat the whole dance from the beginning and continue in this manner until each boy reaches his own partner again. Then, all face about and continue the dance, now progressing around the circle in the opposite direction. When each boy reaches his own partner again and finishes the swing with her, the dance is concluded. This version of the dance is from Häme.

OLD ONE FROM LAUKA—No. 2
(Vanha Laukaalainen)
(Finnish)

Another version of Vanha Laukaalainen is danced in St. Mickel as follows and may be used interchangeably with the Häme version for variety:

A and B.

(**Meas. 1-4, 1-4.**) Any number of couples, each with the girl on the right of her partner, join hands in a ring and circle to the left with sixteen walking steps.

(**Meas. 5-8, 5-8.**) Repeat the same in the opposite direction.

A.

(**Meas. 1-4.**) Partners face each other, join left hands, then with eight walking steps go forward past each other, releasing hands as they go by. On the eighth step all about face to the left.

(**Meas. 1-4.**) All retrace footsteps in the opposite direction, partners giving right hands as they pass each other returning to places.

B.

(**Meas. 5-8, 5-8.**) Again facing each other, partners take left hands and all dance the Chain ("Grand Right and Left") once around the circle until partners meet in their original positions. The "Grand Right and Left" is described in the American country dance **John Brown** on page 3.

A and B.

(**Meas. 1-4, 1-4, 5-8, 5-8.**) Partners join both hands and swing around in place with eight steps, turning in the direction of the hands of the clock. Then releasing hands they pass each other and each boy swings the approaching girl in place turning in the direction opposite to the hands of the clock. Then these two pass each other and each boy swings the next girl, turning in the direction of the hands of the clock, and so on, the boys moving all the way around the circle to the right and the girls to the left, until all reach their original partners. This concludes the dance.

FOLK-DANCES AND SINGING GAMES
GOSSIPING ULLA (Old Man Loikka)
(Finnish)

GOSSIPING ULLA
(Vanha Loikka—Old Man Loikka)
(Finnish)

An even number of dancers form in two parallel lines facing each other about four steps apart, with the boys in one line and their partners in the other line opposite them.

A.

(**Meas. 1-8.**) Beginning with the right foot, all dance eight toe-and-heel steps in place. The toe-and-heel step is as follows: (**Meas. 1.**) With a hop on the left foot, turn to the left and touch the toe of the right foot to the ground toward the opposite line as shown in the illustration (**one**), hop once again on the left foot at the same time facing forward, and place the right heel on the ground forward toward partner (**two**). (**Meas. 2.**) Repeat the toe-and-heel with the other foot, turning to the right and hopping on the right foot. Continue the step alternating left and right in this manner. [Fig. 1.]

B.

(**Meas. 9.**) Beginning with the left foot, partners advance toward each other with two walking steps.

(**Meas. 10.**) Hop forward onto the left foot (**one**), and as they meet, make a quarter-turn to the left so as to face each other, and step sideward to the right past each other, with the right foot (**two**). [Diag. 1.]

(**Meas. 11-12.**) Partners face each other and back away from each other with four walking steps finishing in each other's places. The two lines have now crossed over to exchanged positions.

(**Meas. 13-14.**) The two lines advance and cross over again returning to original positions.

Repeat the whole dance from the beginning and continue in this manner.

Diagram 1

In Uleåborg there is another version of this dance which may be alternated with the above for variety. In this version, **A** is the same as described above. For **B**, however, instead of crossing over, partners join both hands and with eight steps swing around in place turning in the direction of the hands of the clock, then swing around in the other direction with eight steps.

Figure 1

MAY-POLE DANCE—"Bluff King Hal"

(English)

Vivace ♩=80

INTRODUCTION. (ONCE TO YOURSELF.)

MAY-POLE DANCE

The music consists of an Introduction of four measures, and three parts of eight measures each. The Introduction is played only once, while the dancers stand ready to begin the dance. Throughout the entire dance (except as described in the third and fifth steps) the simple skipping step is used.

The dancers in couples form a double circle about the May-pole, all facing in the same direction; Number One in each couple on the left, Number Two on the right. [Diag. 1.]

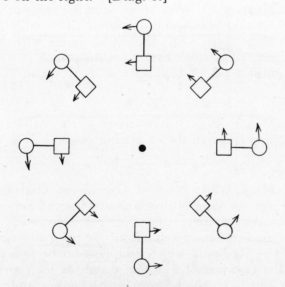

INTRODUCTION
[Once to Yourself]

A. (Meas. 1-4.) With inside hands joined shoulder-high, and girls holding skirts diagonally outward with outside hands, all stand with the weight on the left foot and right foot pointed forward and hold this position through the four measures of the Introduction.

1. A.

(Meas. 1-6.) Beginning, with the right foot, all skip around the pole in a circle, making two skips to each measure.

(Meas. 7-8.) With four skipping steps, the couples swing in facing the pole, and form a single circle with hands joined.

2. B.

(Meas. 1-2.) With four skipping steps, all advance toward the pole, swinging the joined hands forward and up.

(Meas. 3-4.) With four skipping steps, all move back from the pole, lowering the joined hands.

(Meas. 5-8.) Same as Meas. 1-4.

3. C.

(Meas. 1-8.) Join right hands, girls lifting skirts with left hands, and beginning with the right foot turn partners, making two skipping steps to a measure. Finish with Number One inside, with back to the pole and facing partner. [Diag. 2.]

4. A.

(Meas. 1.) Girls lifting their skirts with both hands and beginning with the right foot, Number One and Number Two each polka to the right. In this step each measure should be counted **"one, and, two, and."**

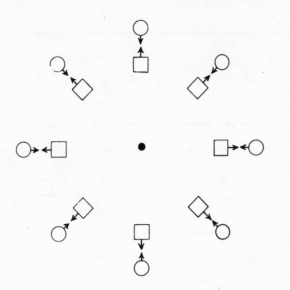

Diagram 2

(**Meas. 2.**) Hop on the right foot and at the same time point the left foot forward and slightly to the left (**one, and**), hop on the right foot, and at the same time touch the left toe behind the right heel (**two, and**).

(**Meas. 3-4.**) Repeat the same, beginning with the other foot and moving to the left.

(**Meas. 5-6.**) Same as Meas. 1-2.

(**Meas. 7-8.**) Same as Meas. 3-4.

5. B.

(**Meas. 1-7.**) Join right hands and turn partners beginning with the right foot, and making one polka-step to a measure. During this step girls' free hand lifts skirt as before.

(**Meas. 8.**) All swing into a single circle, with one more polka-step.

6. C.

(**Meas. 1-8.**) All dance around the circle, beginning with the right foot and making two skipping steps to a measure.

7. A.

(**Meas. 1-2.**) With four skipping steps, all advance toward the pole as in 2 B.

(**Meas. 3-4.**) With four skipping steps, all move back from the pole.

(**Meas. 5-8.**) Same as Meas. 1-4.

8. B-C.

(**Meas. 1-2.**) With four skipping steps, the first couple advance to the pole, and each grasps a ribbon with the right hand.

(**Meas. 3-4.**) With four skipping steps, move backward from the pole to place, and immediately face each other, with the right foot pointed toward partner, Number One turned slightly toward the pole, Number Two turned slightly away from the pole.

(**Meas. 5-8.**) The second couple do the same.

(**Meas. 1-4.**) The third couple do the same.

Continue until all have taken ribbons.

If there are four couples, this will bring them to the eighth measure of C.

9. A-B-C.
Winding the May-pole

(**Meas. 1-24** repeated as necessary.) With skipping steps, all dance a "grand chain," Number Twos moving around the circle from right to left, Number Ones in the opposite direction. The "grand chain" is the same as the "grand right and left" except that the dancers do not take hands but weave their ribbons alternately over and under as they pass each other. This will wind the May-pole and is continued until the ribbons are plaited as far down on the pole as desired. [Diag. 3.]

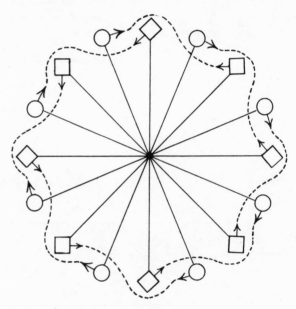

Diagram 3

10. A.

(**Meas. 1-2.**) With four skipping steps all advance to the pole and drop ribbons.

(**Meas. 3-4.**) All join hands, and with four skipping steps move back from the pole.

(**Meas. 5-8.**) Advance and retire again.

11. B.

(**Meas. 1-8.**) Still in a single circle, with sixteen skipping steps all dance around pole.

12. C.

(**Meas. 1-8.**) Number One of the first couple releases the hand of the dancer in front of her. All continue skipping, and Number One leads the dancers in a string away from the pole, all singing.

The May-pole, which is supposed to be dedicated to the Goddess of Flowers, stands at least twelve feet high. Its top is dressed with flowers, and from it hang long streamers (one for each of the dancers) of various light spring colors. Every movement of the dance should be free and joyous, expressive of the sunshine and new life that comes with spring.

STRASÁK

A *Tempo di Polka* ♩ = 128   B. G.

mf

An - nie went to the cab - bage patch, cab - bage patch, cab - bage patch,

And she pick'd the cab - ba - ges up, pick'd the cab - ba - ges up.

Lit - tle Pe - ter came a - long, came a - long, came a - long,

And he kick'd the bas-ket up, kick'd the bas-ket up.

13   14   15   16

B

"You will have to pay for it! You will have to pay for it!"

mf 1   f 2   mf 3   f 4

"No, I won't! No, I won't! I'd ra-ther go to war for it!"

f 5   6   7   8

A

An-nie went to the cab-bage patch, cab-bage patch, cab-bage patch,

mp 1   2   3   4

"No,   I   won't!   No,   I   won't!   I'd   ra - ther   go   to   war   for   it!"

STRAŠÁK

(Czechoslovak)

The Strašák music consists of two distinct strains:—**A,** the first, is repeated, making sixteen measures; **B,** the second, consists of but eight measures.

In fitting the steps to the music, each measure should be counted thus: **"One, and, two, and."**

The dancers form a single circle with partners facing each other. Partners take the ordinary position for round dancing, *i.e.:*—Number One, the man, places right arm around partner's waist.

Number Two, the girl, places left hand on partner's shoulder. Their other hands are joined and held out to the side shoulder high, with arms extended.

Number One begins with the left foot, Number Two with the right.

A.

Couples polka around the circle (moving in the direction opposite to the hands of the clock) left to right turning in the usual way.

The polka is executed on the toes very lightly and breezily. In executing the polka:

(**Meas. 1.**) Number One steps forward with the left foot (**one**), closes the right foot to left (**and**), steps forward with the left (**two**), hops on the left foot (**and**).

(**Meas. 2.**) Repeat the same, beginning with right foot.

(**Meas. 3-16.**) Continue, alternating left foot and right foot.

B.

(**Meas. 1.**) With hands on hips, the dancers stand still facing each other.

(**Meas. 2.**) Dancers stamp vigorously three times; left (**one**), right (**and**), left (**two**), pause (**and**).

(**Meas. 3.**) Dancers stand still.

(**Meas. 4.**) Dancers clap own palms together sharply three times (**one, and, two**), pause (**and**).

(**Meas. 5.**) With left hand on hip, shake right forefinger three times threateningly at partner (**one, and, two**), pause (**and**).

(**Meas. 6.**) With right hand on hip, shake left forefinger three times threateningly at partner (**one, and, two**), pause (**and**).

(**Meas. 7.**) With left hand on hip, strike vigorously with the right hand partner's right hand (**one**). Immediately whirl once around in place to the left on left foot, keeping right foot raised from the ground (**and, two, and**).

(**Meas. 8.**) With hands on hips, and facing partner, stamp three times vigorously in place, beginning with the right foot (**one, and, two**), pause (**and**).

The dance is repeated any number of times desired.

The movements of **A** should be very light and springy, and the dancers should cover as much distance as possible in moving around the circle. During **B,** when the dancers are standing still they should look very fiercely at one another, and all the movements should be vigorous and threatening.

This dance tells the story of an old and popular Bohemian song which is sung during the dance.

KOMARNO

(Bohemian)

B. G.

Tempo di Polka ♩ = 128

KOMARNO

(Czechoslovak)

The Komarno music comprises three parts.

The first, **A,** consists of eight measures; the second, **B,** of four measures; the third, **C,** of twelve measures.

In fitting the steps to the music, each measure should be counted as follows: **"One, and, two, and."**

The dancers form as for "Strasák," but with right hands joined and left hands placed palm out behind the dancer's own waist.

A.

(**Meas. 1.**) Beginning with the left foot, Number One makes a long slide diagonally forward with the left foot (**one**); closes the right foot to the left (**and**); with left foot, makes long slide diagonally forward to the left (**two**); pause (**and**).

(**Meas. 2.**) With the right foot slide diagonally forward to the right (**one**), close the left foot to the right (**and**); with the right foot slide diagonally forward to the right (**two**), pause (**and**).

(**Meas. 3-8.**) Continue the same step, using left foot and right foot alternately.

Number Two at the same time executes the same step with the same foot, but sliding diagonally backward.

B.

(**Meas. 1.**) With the position of the hands still the same, the dancers spring and touch the left foot forward with toes raised from the ground (**one**), pause (**and, two, and**).

(**Meas. 3.**) Dancers spring and change position of feet (**one**), pause in this position (**and, two, and**).

(**Meas. 4.**) Dancers spring and change the position of feet again (**one**); pause in this position (**and, two, and**).

C.

(**Meas. 1-6.**) With left hands still back of own waists, dancers link right elbows, and swing each other with slow running steps, starting with the left foot and making two steps to each measure.

(**Meas. 7-12.**) Releasing right arms, they face the other way, link left arms and swing each other in the opposite direction in the same manner.

At the completion of **C,** dancers resume their original positions and repeat entire dance from beginning. An amusing variety is often added to the dance by each man's quickly seizing another's partner at the completion of **C** and dancing with her, so that there is a continuous change of partners.

TARANTELLA

(Italian)

Arr. by Emma Howells Burchenal

TARANTELLA

(Italian)

The dance as described here is an arrangement of some of the Tarantella steps put into a definite form for convenience in teaching.

The music consists of three parts: **A**, sixteen measures; **B**, the following eight measures; **C**, the last sixteen measures.

In fitting the steps to the music, each measure should be counted thus: **"One, and, two, and."** The dancers form a column of couples, boys on the left, girls on the right. The boys use castanets, a pair in each hand, with the arms curved and raised sideward above shoulder-level; each girl carries a tambourine in the right hand, and beats upon it with the thick lower part of the left palm (or the dancers may, instead, snap fingers and clap hands). During the whole dance they beat time on **"one"** and **"two"** of each measure.

INTRODUCTION

A.

(**Meas. 1-13.**) Beginning with the right foot, and making two steps to a measure, all run forward around the room and up the centre in a straight column. [Diag. 1.]

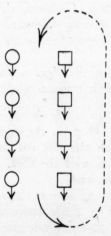

Diagram 1

(**Meas. 14.**) Partners face each other, and run in place.

(**Meas. 15-16.**) Partners make salutation to one another, the girl touching the right toe across behind the left foot and making a curtsey, at the same time extending both arms and raising them slightly to the side.

1. B.

(**Meas. 1-2.**) Beginning with the right foot, all run forward four steps, keeping to the right in passing partners. [Diag. 2.]

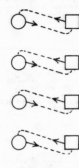

Diagram 2

(**Meas. 3-4.**) With four running steps turn around to the right in place, and face partner.

(**Meas. 5-6.**) With four running steps all cross over again, keeping to the right in passing partners.

(**Meas. 7-8.**) With four running steps turn around to the right in place, and face partner.

2. C.

(**Meas. 1.**) Hop on left foot, and at the same time touch right toe across in front of left (**one, and**); hop on left foot, and at same time touch right toe to the side (**two, and**).

(**Meas. 2-4.**) Continue the same.

(**Meas. 5-8.**) Repeat the same with the left foot.

(**Meas. 9.**) With shoulders and head inclined slightly forward toward partner, and arms lowered, slide sideward with the left foot (**one**), close the right foot to the left (**and**), slide sideward to the left (**two**), close the right foot to the left (**and**).

(**Meas. 10-16.**) Continue sliding to the left, at the same time moving sideward twice around in a circle, keeping face to face with partner and heads close together.

At the end of this figure, partners should find themselves in their original position.

3. A.

(**Meas. 1.**) Hop on the right foot and at the same time touch the left toe forward (**one, and**); change the position of the feet, and touch the left toe forward (**two, and**).

(**Meas. 2-8.**) Continue the same.

(**Meas. 9-16.**) Slide twice around in a circle, same as Meas. 10-16 of the preceding figure, and finish in original position.

4. B.

(**Meas. 1.**) With a spring make a quarter-turn to the right and touch the left toe forward (**one**), rise on both toes (**and**), sink (**two, and**).

(**Meas. 2.**) With a spring make a half-turn to the left, touching the right foot forward (**one**), rise on both toes (**and**), sink (**two, and**).

(**Meas. 3-8.**) Continue turning alternately to right and left.

C.

(**Meas. 1-8.**) Continue the same.

In taking this step, keep face turned toward partner.

(**Meas. 9-16.**) Cross right arm under partner's right arm, and placing left hand behind own waist, grasp partner's right hand with it. With the left foot raised backward, hop on the right foot, making two hops to each measure, and move forward and around, at the same time swinging partner. Finish on the last note with partners side by side in original formation.

INTERLUDE

A.

(**Meas. 1-16.**) In double-column all run forward and partners separate, boys leading off around the room to the left, girls to the right, until they meet at the opposite end of room, when they advance up centre of room in a straight double-column, as before. [Diag. 3.]

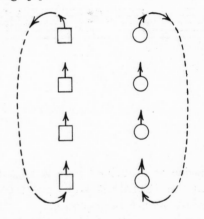

Diagram 3

5. B.

(**Meas. 1-8.**) Same as Meas. 1-8 of first figure.

6. C.

The first two couples now form one set; the third and fourth couples form another set, etc.; and all face toward the centre of their square, so that the boy of one couple faces the girl of the other couple.

(**Meas. 1-8.**) Same as Meas. 1-8 of second figure.

(**Meas. 9-16.**) With heads and shoulders inclined toward the centre of their set, each set slides around to the left as described in Meas. 9-16 of the second figure.

7. A.

(**Meas. 1-8.**) Same as Meas. 1-8 of third figure, but in sets of four.

(**Meas. 9-16.**) Same as Meas. 9-16 of sixth figure.

8. B.

(**Meas. 1-8.**) Same as Meas. 1-8 of fourth figure, but in sets of four.

(**Meas. 1-8.**) With left arms raised slightly higher than shoulder-level, first boy and second girl, and second boy and first girl, join right hands across centre of square (the girls shifting tambourine to left hand). Raise the left foot backward, and hop on the right foot forward and around in a circle making two hops to each measure, the whole set swinging twice around and the girls shaking their tambourines vigorously. [Diag. 4.]

(**Meas. 9-16.**) All face the other way, join hands across centre of square (girls shifting tambourine to right hand), and, hopping on left foot, swing the whole set twice around in the other direction.

The whole dance is very light and exuberant. Toward the end the music should be accelerated, so that the last turn is almost a whirl and the conclusion is quick and bright.

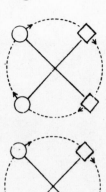

Diagram 4